How to Be Funny

Developing Your Sense of Humor & Funny Comment Delivery

(Tips on How to Be Funny, How to Be Interesting to Men, How to Be Funny)

Williams Winnie

Published By **Simon Dough**

Williams Winnie

All Rights Reserved

How to Be Funny: Developing Your Sense of Humor & Funny Comment Delivery (Tips on How to Be Funny, How to Be Interesting to Men, How to Be Funny)

ISBN 978-1-998038-93-0

No part of this guidebook shall be reproduced in any form without permission in writing from the publisher except in the case of brief quotations embodied in critical articles or reviews.

Legal & Disclaimer

The information contained in this book is not designed to replace or take the place of any form of medicine or professional medical advice. The information in this book has been provided for educational & entertainment purposes only.

The information contained in this book has been compiled from sources deemed reliable, and it is accurate to the best of the Author's knowledge; however, the Author cannot guarantee its accuracy and validity and cannot be held liable for any errors or omissions. Changes are periodically made to this book. You must consult your doctor or get professional medical advice before using any of the suggested remedies, techniques, or information in this book.

Table Of Contents

Chapter 1: Developing Sense Of Humor

A good sense of humor and the ability to make others laugh go hand in hand and neither is possible without the other. It is clinically proved that laughter is the best medicine. Having a good sense of humor is the key to an unending stream of merriment and laughter.

A sense of humor makes you ready for all kinds of situations. You can sail over stressful and tragic circumstances with ease. Getting the bonus of an ideal situation you maximize your give-and-take laughterquota out of it.

There is only benefit to get going on improving your sense of humor. Your life and times could offer you innumerable opportunities of doing so.

Basic approaches to developing your sense of humor

Aim at Perfect Timing: To improve your sense of humor effectively, you must always strive for perfectly timing your comic comments or one-liners. Sometimes in a most serious and intense board meeting your timed interlude would merit guffaws of laughter and immediate lessening of stress, but at some other times, the same effort would merit only fire irritation or condemnation. Perfect timing is necessary for all kinds of situations be it family or office. Along with that the content of you interludes must match the occasion or mismatch it so violently that it creates great fun. Always desist from ethnic or religious content.

Always Keep Smiling: You must keep on smiling to the extent of an aching jaw line or ignoring comments from friends and relatives that you smile too much. You just cannot call it a mere physical feature, because the very action of doing it fills you with a burst of positive energy and your sense of humor waits eagerly for the slightest opportunity to burst out. This also creates magic for all people you encounter, and their positive responses help you further.

Get Rid Of Your Ego:Ego-play can tremendously impair your sense of humor. You must have the quality of being capable of laughing at yourself. Never have the ego that your jokes or one-liners are the most intelligent ones that must evoke laughter from all at all times. If your jokes fall flat sometimes just laugh out heartily yourself and start on a new one or allow the others to come in with theirs. Get rid or minimize your ego to optimize your humor and happiness.

General Intelligence:This is not a binding or restricting requirement. Whatever be your standards of intelligence there are many ways to be practically aware of things happening all around you and your society. Regularly read the newspapers and journals, surf the internet and participate in the social networks, watch samples of TV serials or movies, socialize and attend parties or ceremonies and maintain a healthy interface with your office colleagues. All these will make you intelligent enough to develop a keen sense of humor.

Be An Observer:Following as a corollary from the above point where you embark upon your regular activities your observational prowess can revolutionize your sense of humor. Just look for small details, sidelights, comic flashes, and unique behavioral patterns like ways of laughing out or chatting and the like. Once you start becoming an observer, many more attributes are bound to flood you, and you will have the privilege of adding the choicest ones to your inventory for future use.

How to you develop a healthy Sense of Humor

First of all, you must realize that humor comes from a positive attitude. You must decide in advance to maintain a good attitude despite the adversities you encounter in life. Choosing to remain positive in the midst of a negative situation gives you the personal power to examine situations and circumstances from an objective perspective, which takes unnecessary pressure off of you.

When you can think objectively, you can think clearly, which will allow you to embrace the humor of your situation. When you can laugh at you, you no longer yield power to your circumstance.

Secondly, associate with others who have a healthy sense of humor without being offensive to others. As much as I love to laugh, I am always careful not say anything or say a joke that would offend anyone else. Likewise, I expect the same of others I communicate with. There is no joy in humor if it offends others. That is one of the quickest ways to make enemies and develop a bad reputation.

Thirdly, A relatively easy way to engage in humor is to keep up with the latest buzz and things that are trending. This includes catching up on the latest memes, satire and silly news stories.

Having a good sense of humor is not only about being able to make others laugh but also being able to understand witty jokes yourself. Being informed about what's trending and what will help you avoid a faux pas when you find yourself staring ignorantly after someone cracks a joke about a silly trend like Owling or Horsemanning.

Fourthly, Humor can be better understood by knowing the differences in various cultures, ethnicities or the lifestyles of people who are different from others. In the day and age of multicultural workplaces, schools, and colleges, it is vital to be fairly informed about the idiosyncrasies of different cultures and ethnic backgrounds. Exposure to different cultures, typical behavior, their customs, their habits and culinary styles will also help you draw the line between humor and things that are considered offensive.

Fifth, Whenever someone around you tells a funny story, cracks a joke or shares a humorous experience, look beyond the laughter and spot the intricacies of what it took for them to make everyone laugh. From body language to voice tone pick up tips on how someone was able to sustain humor in a conversation. Create a pool of learning, experiences, and slices of life as you meet and interact with different characters. Draw inspiration from their funny side and incorporate bits of it into your behavior to showcase your sense of humor in its full glory.

Sixth, Exercise discretion in picking the right type of TV shows or movies to watch and broaden your humor horizon. Avoid too many Chaplinesque slapstick or cheesy romantic comedies. Instead focus on films and TV shows that play on intelligent, sarcastic, witty and subtle humor.

From Woody Allen films to Chris Rock characters, from Monty Python and the Holy Grail films to Little Miss Sunshine type alternative and witty cinema, try to soak in a wide range of humor. Well written iconic TV shows like The Big Bang Theory, Friends, South Park, Everybody Loves Raymond, Seinfeld and The Simpsons are rife with plots that show how everyday mundane situations can be infused with wit and humor.

Seventh, Watching stand-up comedy is an invaluable way to learn the about the body language associated with humor and satire. Witnessing humor live is all about sensing the reaction and pulse of an audience. By being a part of a live performance, it is easier to understand the finer nuances of what makes people smile, smirk, tickle or bend over with laughter.

If your city or town does not play host to stand-up comedy nights, the acts of international comedy maestros like Adam Hills, Bill Cosby, Kathy Griffin, Russell Peters, Dane Cook, Larry the Cable Guy or their likes can also be seen on YouTube or DVD.

Eighth, One of the prerequisites for having a great sense of humor is to be able to laugh at oneself. A certain amount of lightness in the heart and transparency in character makes it much easier to absorb humor. Being too uptight in social scenarios, expecting others to behave in a particular way or taking offense easily can become roadblocks in understanding humor.

Laughing at yourself will arm you with the ability to decipher between things that are funny and the things that are dull and boring. It will also help you draw the line between being sarcastically funny and sounding rude.

Ninth, Creating original humor is more about picking up incidents from everyday life and giving them a comic twist. In mundane everyday situations, humor may not lie explicitly on the surface. But its true value is showcased when someone has the sense and understanding to point it out.

Observing everyday situations can be as simple as watching how passengers behave while commuting on a train, the expressions they make and the kind of banter they engage in.

Soon enough, you will get into the habit of effortlessly plucking out the comical and funny side of situations that may seem mundane on the surface.

Tenth, Sticky conversations and awkward situations are not the best places to be in, but they can be made easier with a dash of witty humor, which also serves as a good icebreaker. The trick is to think on your feet and say something funny without being offensive.

Pull out a humorous trump card from the repertoire of witty anecdotes that you may have experienced yourself. Use them as a tool to steer and manipulate conversations your way. The art of getting out of awkward situations with funny lines is part and parcel of having a good sense of humor.

Benefits of Developing a good Sense of Humor

If you have an interest in enhancing your health, brain, social life, and state of mind, attempt to laugh more. Having a good sense of humor is beneficial to several elements of your life. A well-developed sense of humor has incredible advantages. Chuckling and smiling aren't frivolous activities. So, stop being so serious and discover why humor is so important.

A sense of humor has numerous benefits:

1.Reduce stress

Day-to-day living can be pretty demanding. There are lots of ways to relieve tension. However few feel as good as a good laugh. With a common sense of humor, it's easy to find various reasons to laugh about life. A great laugh will permit you to forget your difficulties for a little while.

2.Increase your intelligence

At the minimum, you'll learn more quickly. A study demonstrated that laughing stimulates the learning centers of the brain. Promoting those areas regularly is believed to boost the ability to learn and retain new information. Laughing might assist you to get a scholarship to Harvard.

3.Reinforce your health

The more you laugh, the less regularly you'll be sick. Studies have revealed that laughing enhances the body's immune system. It likewise decreases your risk of high blood pressure, which is great for your heart and brain. It's possible that laughter can lower your medical costs.

4.Boost your social life

Whether you're trying to find brand-new friends or searching for the man or woman of your dreams, having a funny bone, or sense of humor, is important. Think about the most popular people you know. Are they upbeat and do they smile easily? Or do they do not have a good sense of humor?

5.A funny bone is attractive

Who does not like to laugh? We're instinctively drawn to individuals that laugh easily. Everybody wants to have fun and release their stress.

If you're enjoyable to be with and you understand ways to make others laugh, you'll find yourself surrounded by others who likewise have a common sense of humor.

6.Boost your mood

It feels great to laugh, and the good feelings can last for hours afterward. Humor can reroute your focus from the negative happenings in your life to something more pleasurable.

7.Reinforce your relationships

Is it possible to have a relationship that would not take advantage of your sense of humor? Laughing together will bring you closer. You'll find that your relationships with your neighbors, pals, family, and coworkers take advantage of your ability to laugh and appreciate the lighter side of life.

8.Benefit others

Your state of mind, words, and actions affect those around you. When you're in a bad mood, it adversely affects others. Your smiling, pleased face and state of mind are uplifting and lighten up the moods of those around you.

9.Laughing is good for you

Your sense of humor affects your health, the state of mind, social life, and those around you. They say that "Laughter is the best medicine." Now you have a better understanding as to why that statement is true. Discover the humor in life and keep your state of mind light. There are no benefits to expecting the worst and experiencing negative moods.

Spend time with others who take pleasure in laughing. Make it a point to take pleasure in funny movies or watch your favorite comics. Your laughter helps you and those around you. Feel free to laugh more.

Chapter 2: Bad Sense Of Humor

Some people don't laugh much even if there is something to laugh about. Others seem to be chuckling to themselves all the time. People who can laugh at themselves are a lot more fun to be around because you feel they don't take themselves too seriously, so you don't need to either.

Some people are always laughing and finding stuff to laugh about. They watch Tom and Jerry, they love comedies, they go to comedy shows, and they like to laugh.

People with Asperger Syndrome for example, often have no sense of humor and don't laugh at themselves. They don't laugh much at all. Asperger Syndrome often means; Rage, tantrum, shutdown, self-isolating reactions appearing "out of nowhere."

Signs You Have a Bad Sense of Humor

•You don't make laugh a priority

As the old saying goes, "life's better when you're laughing, " and no one knows that more than good-humored individuals. Those who have a bad sense of humor don't see the value in making others laugh, even to prioritize their laughter. And as a result, they are not healthier and not happier for it: Studies show that those who doesn't put on smiling decreases their mood and increase tension and stress.

•You don't practice self-acceptance

Bad humored individuals do not embrace their flaws and laugh them off (and let them go) in a healthy way. Self-acceptance is a key to a happier life, but it's not always practiced all that often.

•You're not creative

It takes a lot of mental energy to come up with quick-witted quips that keep grins on others' faces. Those who have a bad sense of humor tends not to be more creative.

•You have bad physical well-being

Laughter truly is the best medicine — and people who have a good sense of humor use it to their advantage. Those giggles can stimulate the organs, improve your immune system and relieve pain.

•People often wonder if you're joking or are serious

Because your jokes have no punch line, and often don't sound like jokes, people will question whether you are serious or not.

•You say funny things with a serious, calm expression

You keep a straight face at all times throughout your jokes. Your expressions are monotone, and sometimes you'll give a smirk here and there. But for the most part, you look mad, or depressed.

Chapter 3: Improve Your Sense Of Humour

Humor helps reduce the stress and strengthen the immune system helping an individual to overcome any pain with utmost ease. Humour also brings relationships to life. Without it, most relationships become lifeless and meaningless.

Humour isn't a thing that can be defined with specific words. Humour is different to different people. But making an offensive joke and expecting the audience to laugh over it isn't human.

Some people think that they are funny while they are only talking senseless things which do not entertain anyone, instead only irritate others. Being witty is about talking and laughing with dignity and at the same time offering light and cheerful moments to the people around. There are many factors that decide how humorous you are.

How To Improve Your Sense Of Humour

•Learn to laugh at yourself

When your start to laugh at your situations, others begin to laugh with you too. Try to find humor in some of the most embarrassing moments you remember from the past and learn to tell them like stories with a funny side added. Be dramatic while telling your stories and exaggerate a bit to add the element of humor.

•Self-deprecation will slowly become a way you create a light environment around you and open yourself to humorous aspects of your life

As you learn to see life in a different light positively and humorously, you shall learn to make humor in most situations. Be sure not to make fun out of stories that are personal or make the crowd uncomfortable.

•Try to laugh at annoying or frustrating situations

Certain situations annoy you or spoil your mood. A sudden fall amidst a crowd, a hole discovered in your favorite shirt that you are just about to wear for a party or your step landings into dog poop, etc are some situations where you are likely to get angry. It is expected about how you feel and thus very normal for you to act annoyed. But the fact is that nothing is achieved, or nothing can be changed about what has been done. There is an easy yet funny way to get out of such situations.

•Try to imagine someone you like or extremely dislike in your situation

Keep imagining the faces that come to your mind until you feel that you have thought of the best person to experience your predicament. This will bring a laugh on his state and then you shall eventually laugh on yourself.

Another way is to recollect the unfortunate events of the day and laugh in the mirror over the accidents and falls that happened. It will help you not feel frustrated over the situations and is an effective way not to lose temper.

•Get back your smile

A smile is very synonymous with a laugh, though technically they are different things. There are many things in this world that demand a smile. A toddler's activities and talks, lush green surroundings with chirping birds, a task completed successfully at work or home, the news of a friend or loved one coming, watching a funny movie or humorous serial are just a few examples.

A person who smiles often is more likely to feel less burdened with the pressures of work and life and hence revive his/her sense of humor. The absence of smile is considered as a state of depression or stress where a person misses many joys of life.

•Read Comics and joke books often

Cut out the jokes from joke books that make you laugh the most and put them on the notice board or on some place like your office table where they are on your horizon.

Frequently seeing those jokes and comics will help you feel relaxed. Even if you read more comics, it has a very positive influence on your humor and helps enhance the humorous outlook you keep towards situations in life.

•Watch Comedy shows

Watch the late night popular comedy shows where hosts and comedians make everyone laugh with their well-timed and humorous talks. Their expressions and style must be noted to see and understand what is it that makes people laugh every time they mark a statement. It is the way they put forth funny statements that make them more interesting, and you find them humorous. You can even use their one-liner jokes in your talks and try to note how people react.

•Listen to funny stories about friends and colleagues

When you meet friends or colleagues at workplace ask them to tell you some funny things of past week that happened to them. Listening to humorous true stories is far better than hearing to gossip, and people will remember you as someone who has a penchant for humor.

Once you develop the habit of talking and laughing over funny sides of real incidents, you will inculcate an attitude of humor and laughter within you.

•Overstate problems

The more we exaggerate our problems to make fun out of them, the humorous perspective towards life and situations enhances. As they say, the problem is only as big as you want to see it; similarly the problem is as serious or funny as you look at it. The more fun you seek in exaggerating a problem when talking about it to someone, the lighter and dramatic the problem becomes with it being told as a tale with twists and turns.

Thus, it makes you feel as if the problem is a drama and you are supposed to laugh at it and not take it to heart.

•Do something humorous each day

You are what you do. So if you want to become a person with an improved sense of humor, you ought to make it a routine. Do something silly each day. Make one humorous activity a part of your To-Do List, and mark it only when you accomplish it. Humor experts think that if you manage to include humor as a part of your tasks, you shall automatically regain or develop a humorous attitude.

•Enjoying stand up gigs

Stand-up gigs are essential to understanding how people feel about the jokes. When you create an atmosphere to enjoy them, you shall develop a perspective of what makes you laugh and what kind of humor is personally funny for you.

Even watching comedy movies or comedy shows on T.V. can help you laugh over situations and in turn, help seeks humor in situations which you normally fail to find funny.

•Don't go overboard with humor

Finding humor in awkward and offensive situations isn't the right way to have fun. If you try to force humor into situations, it will only ruin your image as a person, and people will try to stay away.

Humour has to come naturally. You don't have to overdo it at social situations or plan it as it can become forced in such a case. Humour is spontaneous and unplanned, and that is why it makes people laugh in the most.

•Share fun with family

Any time you sit with your family members for dinner or supper, make sure that you share your funny moments of the day with them. Sharing some light moments with family will reduce your stress levels and bring a cheerful and humorous person out of you who does not see the embarrassment in things that go wrong in life but instead seeks fun and humor in it. You cannot change the situations or occasional things that happen to you any day, but you can become a more happy-go-lucky person by taking them in a fun-filled manner.

•Spend time with children

Children love fun and have the attitude of finding humor in small things. Spending time with children can give you the sense of seeking fun in strange situations which you take very normally otherwise.

A light-hearted approach is an alternate perspective that you can learn from children's humor that can be refreshing and different from occasional jokes that are developed for adults. Remember that humor isn't about finding some mature stuff to laugh over. You can simply have a good sense of humor with a genuine and heart-felt smile to cherish. Others will also see the purity in your humor.

•Laugh and make others laugh

As you learn to find fun in your situations and see how it eliminates the undue pressure that you face every day, most of your worries and stress fades away with a heart-felt laughter. Laughing may have to be practiced, to begin with until it becomes a part of your personality.

People who laugh often are counted as socially active and tend to succeed with their attitude and sense of humor. Your laugh will remove the toxins that you can never get rid of with any physical exercise or any diet.

Conclusion

Mark Twain has rightly said,

"But laughing has natural wonders on your body and mind which cannot be neglected. Our mistakes become trivial when we shoo them away with a laugh."

People who laugh often are more confident and have lesser insecurities and fears in life. You shall find yourself more competent and capable with a smile around the corners of your mouth.

The sense of humor can be developed as easily as any other skill in life and bring a positive change in your life and relationship. We are confident that following this humor kind day- by- day makes you a more charismatic person with an enhanced sense of humor.

PART TWO

IMPLEMENTING OF SENSE OF HUMOR

"Humor can make a serious difference. In the workplace, at home, in all areas of life — looking for a reason to laugh is necessary. A sense of humor helps us to get through the dull times, cope with the difficult times, enjoy the good times and manage the scary times." — Steve Goodier

Chapter 4: Implementing Humor At Workplace

Despite the belief that business is serious, humor can lighten the mood within organizational environments and make working life more enjoyable. Humor is a very common, but understudied phenomenon at work. Within work groups, which are fundamentally driven by the rules of human interaction, understanding the multifunctional role of humor in organizations can contribute to effective management of personnel. Indeed, the proper use of organizational humor can provide valuable benefits to organizations and even more valuable tools to management for motivating staff, communicating effectively, and mitigating discord.

Humor itself is comprised of many facets and styles. Often considered only informally as an approach for communicating levity, there is a science to humor, one that can be effectively applied as a serious tool for managers and leaders within organizations. It can be used for more than simply joking and laughing or building camaraderie; it can serve as a toolkit, complete with a range of specific tools that can be selectively used and applied by management.

Hodge-Cronin & Associates in their survey found that of 737 CEOs surveyed, 98 percent preferred job candidates with a sense of humor to those without. Another survey indicated that 84 percent of the executives thought that employees with a sense of humor do a better job than people with little or no sense of humor.

Dr. David Abramis at Cal State Long Beach has studied fun at work for years. He's discovered that people who have fun on the job are more creative, more productive, better decision-makers, and get along better with co-workers. They also have fewer absentee, late, and sick days than people who aren't having fun.

The benefits to a pleasant and happy workplace are that happy employees are more loyal and productive employees. The absenteeism and tardiness rate may decrease as people look forward to going to work. The turnover rate may decrease, as employees feel content and loyal to an organization. And the cost associated with illness may decrease as people experience the positive physiological and psychological effects of laughter.

Reasons Why Humour in the Workplace is Important

Humor and work have always had a tenuous relationship, albeit one that has softened in recent years. Even in the most casual office environments, there are certain stigmas and uncertainties surrounding humor.

There are several compelling reasons why judicious use of humor can help your workplace become happier and more productive at workplace.

1. Humor helps morale

As you'd expect, a workplace which feels fun and friendly to be in is one that will encourage happy employees. Morale is directly linked with motivation, so it's in every manager's interests to encourage high morale. If a little levity smooths that path, all the better!

2. Humor helps your career

The research on this is compelling: in a Robert Half International Survey, a staggering 91% of executives who responded felt that a sense of humor was important for career advancement, and 84% agreed that someone with a good sense of humor does a better job. Humour makes you appear calm and in control of a situation, and able to look at it with perspective, imbuing you with a greater air of authority. Whether you're in a managerial position or just looking to step up the ladder, a well-timed piece of humor can only help your chances.

3.Laughter Lowers Blood Pressure and Improves Blood Flow

Not only does laughter help your immune system, but it also has an effect on your cardiovascular system. Laughter can lower your heart rate, reduce your blood pressure and even improve the function of your blood vessels; laughter causes an expansion of your endothelium (the tissue that forms the inner lining of your blood vessels), which improves blood flow and even reduces your chances of cardiovascular disease.

4.Supervisors Who Use Humor Are Perceived as Better Leaders

Leaders who integrate humor as part of their management style are not only proven to foster greater work performance, satisfaction, and cohesion amongst workers; they are perceived as better leaders and managers. Subordinates also report experiencing greater work satisfaction when working with managers who integrate humor in their interactions.

5.Humor helps your health

'Laughter is the best medicine,' they say, and it is certainly true that laughing has been linked with both short and long term health benefits. Laughing stimulates the heart and lungs, increases blood flow around the body and increases feel-good endorphins released from the brain. It can also increase your ability to cope with difficult situations or break the ice to prevent a potential conflict.

6.Humour breaks down barriers

It's perhaps not surprising that most of us feel more comfortable sharing a joke with a co-worker than our boss; the risk of a superior taking your humor the wrong way is greater than someone with no power over you. But a shared joke establishes common ground and lessens the perception of the difference between people. Research shows that where someone is telling a compelling story, the storyteller and their listeners are mirroring one another's brain patterns and fostering connections that strengthen their bond.

7.Humor Boosts Creative Thinking

Humor has been proven to help develop creative thinking in various settings. Not only does it provide a more colorful environment, but a playful office also helps encourage openness and diminish the fear of criticism towards outlandish or creative ideas. Even people who don't share their humor at the office are more relaxed about speaking up in settings where levity is encouraged.

8.Humor Is More Important Than Pay

An industry-wide study of over 2,500 people found that 55% of workers would take less pay to have more fun at work. This means a majority of people would take a pay cut for a more light-hearted work environment.

9.Humorous Advertisements Are More Effective

On the marketing side, humor has been proven to make advertisements more memorable and increase the likelihood of the viewer taking action. Studies measuring advertisement awareness found that ads with humor had nearly 25% greater impact across the board.

10.A Sense of Humor Reduces Sick Days

Laughter boosts your immune system by enhancing your antibodies (which help fight infections) and increasing your immune cell count. This helps reduce your chances of illness and missing out on work.

11.Joking Around Does Not Distract People From Work

Worried that office humor will lead to distraction? Studies show increased humor in the workplace does not detract from people's productivity or their ability to complete tasks that require concentration.

12.Fun Environments Reduce Burnout and Turnover

Not surprisingly, humor in the workplace has been proven to enhance worker's coping mechanisms and reduce worker withdrawal and burnout. It has also been shown to improve employee retention and reduce overall rates of attrition.

How To Add Humorous Laughter To Your Workplace

Tactics to adding more humor to your workplace interactions:

•Create a sense of belonging

Comedy is often a conspiracy: if you can poke light fun at outsiders (think competitors), you're well on your way to building a strong rapport with your team.

•Be authentic and honest

This might be the most important tactic. Emotionally disarming people are naturally funny.

Make fun of your company/department/yourself But without diminishing it (that's true self-confidence!).

•Integrate surprise into your monthly or🔲uarterly meetings

It's not always easy, but it is possible. "Whether we prefer cubicles or crusades, embracing the unpredictable adds vibrancy to our experience, deepens our relationships, improves our ability to adapt to change, and lets us make a greater impact on others," says Tania Luna, co-author of the book Surprise: Embrace the Unpredictable and Engineer the Unexpected. Isn't that something we all want for our teams?

•Avoid interrupting or offending

This takes practice, but once your team sees you behaving in a light-hearted but respectful manner, they'll follow suit, which creates a culture of respect and openness.

•Allow people to be accepted as they are

A recent article in New York Magazine highlighted how Google found the benefits of psychological safety to be key to team effectiveness. The whole article is worth a read, but basically, when people feel free to be who they are without judgment or ridicule, they feel more comfortable being funny.

Chapter 5: Sense Of Humor In The Classroom

Humor is a valuable teaching tool for establishing a classroom climate conducive to learning. Humor as a pedagogical tool can be like walking a tightrope. If done well, it could enhance learning or at the very least make learning more fun. Appropriate and timely humor in the college classroom can foster mutual openness and respect and contribute to overall teaching effectiveness. However, if not done well, it could have disastrous consequences. I remember a few years ago attending a webinar on the use of humor, and I found it to be so ineffective and boring that it was funny.

Humor in educational settings serves a variety of positive functions beyond simply making people laugh. Humor builds group (as in class) cohesion. People respond more positively to each other when humor is present. It brings them together. Humor can facilitate cohesion by softening criticism.

Research also establishes that humor helps individuals cope with stress. It relaxes them. But not all the functions of humor are positive. If humor is used divisively or to disparage others, it weakens group cohesion. Humor has negative impacts when it is used as a means of control. For example, given the power dynamic in the classroom, it is highly inappropriate for instructors to target students by making fun of their ignorance or beliefs.

There are many different types of humor that have been identified, among the humor which relates to class material, funny stories (hopefully related to the content), humorous comments, self-disparaging humor, unplanned humor (spontaneous, unintentional), jokes, riddles, puns, funny props, and visual illustrations. Humor related to course material, funny stories, and humorous comments are almost always appropriate. Other kinds of humor are appropriate depending on the context. And some kinds of humor are never appropriate, such humor that manipulates, denigrates, ridicules, or mocks others and offensive humor that is racially or sexually based.

Research has documented that the use of humor can benefit educational instructors in a couple of important ways.

•Create a Comfortable Learning Environment

When teachers share a laugh or a smile with students, they help students feel more comfortable and open to learning. Using humor brings enthusiasm, positive feelings, and optimism to the classroom.

"Because I know that a good laugh eases tension, increases creativity, I will do almost anything to get the class rolling with laughter voice inflections, exaggerated facial expressions and movements, hilarious personal stories (of which I have way too many), ridiculous example and I encourage my students to do the same."

Even if you're not naturally funny, you still can lighten things up a bit. The key thing to remember is to do what's comfortable for you. Not only will it make you more approachable, but it will also help put students more at ease in your classroom.

•Fire Up Their Brains

During her research on learning and humor, educator-researcher Mary Kay Morrison looked at brain scans that showed high levels of activity in multiple areas of the brain when humor was used in conversation and instruction.

"We're finding humor lights up more of the brain than many other functions in a classroom," says Morrison, author of Using Humor to Maximize Learning. "In other words, if you're listening just auditorily in a classroom, one small part of the brain lights up, but humor maximizes learning and strengthens memories."

•Bring Content to Life

Teachers can use humor to bring content to life— through games, parody, or comical voices (or wigs or hats). Students respond to their teacher's playfulness and appreciate the effort he or she puts into making a lesson fun.

Guidelines for Teaching with Humor

1.Make humor relevant

Humor in the classroom is most effective when linked to concepts being studied. Humor that educates will help in becoming a more effective instructor. A three-step method exists for delivering content-relevant humor (Polio, 2001). The instructor first explains the content information without humor. The humorous example, demonstration, or activity then follows the explanation. Finally, the instructor summarizes the information and how it relates to the humorous event.

2.Don't be afraid to be funny

Students often resist asking questions because they fear embarrassment. If the instructor shows no fear of embarrassment and models that learning the information is paramount, this modeling creates an atmosphere where students will take a chance and get involved.

3.Humor should not be hurtful

Humor is something that's not hurtful, and everyone can laugh at. The humor is non-hostile and non-derisive of others. When considering the use of humor an instructor needs to consider the subject, tone, intent, and the situation.

The subject – considering what students have experienced can help decide what subject matter lends itself to appropriate humor. There are subjects that are off-limits for humor.

Tone – Teachers need to be conscious of their level of sarcasm as too much sarcasm may turn off students who believe the instructor is too negative. If students cannot distinguish between sarcasm and seriousness, students may become confused or offended.

Intent — Before using humor, it is wise to consider if the usage will alienate or embarrass any of the students. The intent of adding humor is to facilitate learning.

4.Act it out

When an instructor is without audio/ visuals, another strategy is to "act it out." The benefit of acting it out gives the instructor the ability to stop at any moment and ask questions. By acting out the situation and risking the embarrassment the students are more willing to engage in the question and answer session that follows.

5.Use clips from movies or television shows

By linking course information to popular shows, the students have a greater chance to retain the course material. Another option is to have the students identify and bring in movie clips, or find youtube.com clips of the material being taught.

6.Classroom Management

Instead of becoming annoyed with students whose phones go off, or at students who are using their computers for other reasons. Identify a way to stop the behavior through humor.

7.Test and Quizzes

Inputting a humorous question in an exam or quiz can relax a student and help ease test anxiety and improve performance.

8.Use yourself as an example

Sharing a personal story or demonstrating a personal experience and tying it to the course material opens up discussion in the class and the potential for students to share their experiences.

9.Use stories and comments from students

Using student examples can help open up a class early in a semester. Sharing a story or two from past classes or semesters, it sends the message that it is appropriate and desired that students interact and share in class.

10.Be yourself

Instructors need to find an application of humor that fits who they are. Choose what might work for a particular teaching style.

The use of humor in the classroom, when used effectively, can result in some benefits for both the instructor and student.

PART THREE

HUMOR AND LIFE

What is life without a sense of humor? Man would be nothing but a reasoning animal without it. Many a life has been inspired by the ability to laugh in a tough situation and smile at the miseries of life. The drudgery of life is often relieved by these little glorious moments of humor. The capacity to see the flip side of life in the day to day situations and to come out of the bottlenecks of life, with a smile is indeed a great blessing, a great gift of the Gods. Charlie Chaplin had often said that he would not have survived the greatest battles of his life without the great sense of humor he had. He could come out smiling in the hardest moments of his life. He laughed at the ironies of life, the very bitter sarcasm that life is.

Oscar Wilde, P.G.Wodehouse, and many great authors, great humor writers- all of them did suffer greatly in life, but their sense of humor saved the day for them. Life and the drudgeries of everyday living cannot be changed by crying or crimping about it. What next is the big question? In this question for solutions, if one can keep a cool head by being sensible and light-hearted about the situation, definitely the chances are that solutions would emerge on its own. Gloominess, depression, and melancholy can only add miseries to life. But humor can brighten life, inspire the mind and spark the brain to look for way outs. That is why the sense of humor is a must for healthy living.

Look at all the successful personalities. The vagaries of life never fazed them. They overcame the vicissitudes of life through hard work and the ability to see the lighter side.

Progress in life can be achieved through these qualities only. The depressed man never did go very far. Robert Bruce would have given up long back if he had no will to succeed and the ability to look beyond the seemingly gloomy and murky impasse.

Chapter 6: The Need For Sense Of Humour In Life

Life is complex enough in itself. Our duty is to make it as fun and pleasant as it can be even in adversity. I believe, one must have a sense of humor to carry through and lighten the burden of our everyday mental stress. Otherwise, life's trying times could drown us in self-pity and bitterness. Life is too short. To cry over spilled milk not only stalls you but takes away the joy of our experience in life.

We are subjected to trivial and significant challenges every day, but the way we choose to respond to them is what will make the difference. To a certain extent, one has the power to make the best out of the worst situation, just by tackling it with a sense of humor. Is a reminder of the adage that says, "If life throws you lemons, make yourself a lemonade." Along with my life's journey, I realized that regardless of any given situation's status, the psychological burden that comes with it is easier to deal with if is taken with a sense of humor. Living life is a serious business. But if we see things from the bright perspective even when there isn't one, it will help you fell less stressed during your sad moments.

Perhaps, approaching our daily life's endeavors with a sense of humor has a lot to do in triggering our endorphins. This makes us feel mentally happier or stable. Whether this is true or not, no one would refute the fact that having a sense of humor at least makes you a more likable person. Conse⬚uently, yielding better results in our everyday interaction with other people, such as loved ones, co-workers or a potential employer.

Adding Humor to Your Life

Why is adding a little humor in your life helpful? That's because it eases your mind a great deal, lifting off pressures from your shoulders, helping you to lead a happy and healthy life while you carry out daily tasks smoothly and even enjoy doing them.

Below are tips on how you can add humor to your life

I.When you are grumpy and gloomy, it will only lead to more mishaps and disasters. Why not curve your lips in the form of a smile and then actually smile? Immediately your sense of humor is turned on and who knows you may burst out laughing.

II.Examine yourself in front of a full-length mirror from head to toe. What are the things you like about yourself? What do you dislike? For example, it's your nose you dislike, and it's your hair you like. Appreciate what you like and joke about what you dislike in your features. For instance, you can say, "I am so thankful for my beautiful hair, but I dislike the way my nose looks - that's OK, and I can still live up to it. Is it that bad? Nobody ever said so. So I am only making it up! Ha ha!!" Lighten up and smile. The moment you smile in front of the mirror, you are going to burst into happy laughter. That's when you make your day.

III.Read a jokes book or surf the net to find a handful of jokes to read. Laugh heartily. That's what life should be like. You should enlighten yourself all the time, without letting yourself becoming too serious.

IV.Share the good jokes you know with your colleagues during break time and break out into fun laughter. You will immediately win over a lot of hearts, who will like you very much. So why not do it more often?

V.Share a funny anecdote about an incident involving your son or daughter with a friend face-to-face or on the phone. Make it as funny as you can so that it makes your friend smile and laugh. Let him share his funny life anecdotes with you and laugh and laugh again. That's how life should be.

VI.Dress up funny like a clown and play pranks on your kids. You kids will love the fun and have a very good laugh. These are the moments to savor, and along with them you will also smile and laugh.

VII.How about your significant other? Has everything become monotonous and routine-like for them? Why don't you find something honest to compliment them? For example, you can say, "You look smart in your new hair cut!!" It will cheer them up and make them smile.

VIII.Tell a joke. No, seriously. Tell a joke. I don't care if you have never told a joke in your life, or if you claim that you cannot tell a joke to save your life. You're wrong... Just tell a joke. You don't have to tell it well; you just have to do it. I promise you: when you think about jokes, when you think about humor, and when you think about fun... fun will follow.

IX.Linger over the funny pages. Notice -- and enjoy -- the fact that you are doing nothing but thinking about humor, laughter, and fun. Give yourself permission to linger and enjoy it. As I said above, think about humor and humor WILL follow.

X.Pick up a book about fun, humor, and laughter. It might be a funny book (like the Dave Barry books or maybe the comic Doonesbury books). Find a book about humor that intrigues you and commits a few minutes each day to reading about laughter.

XI.Spend time with upbeat people who make you laugh. You get juice from those people, don't you? This time focus on giving them some energy back. Be an upbeat, fun, excited, exciting, interested, interesting person yourself. That way you both end up leaving with more joy for the day. Nothing can draw out your best YOU more than fun people whom you admire.

How to Use Humor to Change Your Life

The paradigm is simple. You must believe in your thoughts and essentially in the power of your mind. You want to change, right! Today, I'm referring to another way to use positive affirmations. I've written before about positive affirmations being an effective tool to change yourself. Since I believe that it is one of the simplest yet most effective tools to change it can't be overstated. What I am now suggesting is using humor.

Imagine everything as funny, funny enough to laugh at yourself. Do you want to lose weight? How about seeing yourself as the laughing Buddha even as you pat your fat belly and tell yourself that your belly is going to disappear now. See it happen as you become the skinny Buddha. Keep the wide open grin and bubbly eyes. By repeating this one image as you continue your diet program, the added stimulus will help you lose weight. After all, your very positive feelings (humor) as you follow your mental image of your future thinness is a great motivator toward reaching your goal.

By seeing yourself as the skinny Buddha, you merely say to yourself. "I will become the skinniest Buddha alive." Make sure it happens. Some people who want to see themselves as thin in the future as they continue their diet imagine themselves like a snake, a piece of rope, as the fattest person alive and then in a flash whittle themselves down to become a string bean. They are incorporating imagery into their affirmation.

Affirmations make you act differently. You see yourself differently. You begin to act to fulfill your desires. And as you feel success you will add new affirmations. They only take a few seconds to repeat, and you can do them several or more times a day, every day. You will soon see yourself as a very positive person. But with this approach make the affirmations funny. If you see yourself as creative, then create the oddest looking creative anteater or multicolored baboon you can imagine.

Although for most people positive affirmations should be realistic, others believe in wild exaggeration. They see themselves as the most creative person alive, the greatest cook, the fastest reader, the greatest poet, the greatest of anything, knowing fully well that the exaggeration is to spur them to change. If exaggerations, especially when embellished with humor, appeal to you, try them. You have nothing to lose. You can always return to a more realistic approach. But experimentation can open a new vista in your search for ways to change your life.

You have nothing to lose by trying them. You will be more enthusiastic, more playful, more humorous, and more optimistic as your positive thoughts guide you. Try it and keep it up.

One day you'll be surprised to find that you lost a few pounds if your affirmation was about dieting. Or you have more energy and vitality if your affirmation was about exercise or eating breakfast. You have begun to follow your affirmations, and inner changes are occurring. And these changes become the impetus for further change. And repeating affirmations is fun, kind of like talking to yourself as you skip down the street.

You can rapidly and effectively expand your creative life by following the methods and exercises described in "Awakening Your Creativity." In this book, you will find the primary tools to change your life in ways that will excite and delight you. You can become creative.

Chapter 7: Using Your Sense Of Humor In Romantic Relationships

We've all heard that laughter is the best medicine, and it's true. Laughter relieves stress, elevates mood, enhances creativity, and makes you more resilient. But it's not just good for your emotional and physical health. It's also good for your relationships. Laughter brings people closer together and creates intimacy. And it's an especially powerful tool for managing conflict and reducing tension when emotions are running high. Whether with romantic partners, friends, and family, or co-workers, you can learn to use humor and play to smooth over disagreements, lower everyone's stress level, and communicate in a way that builds up the relationships rather than breaking it down.

The Role Of Humor And Laughter In Relationships

Humor plays an important role in all kinds of relationships. In new relationships, humor can be an effective tool not just for attracting the other person but also for overcoming any awkwardness or embarrassment that arises during the process of getting to know one another. In established relationships, humor can keep things exciting, fresh, and vibrant. It can also help you get past conflicts, disagreements, and the tiny aggravations than can build up over time and wreck even the strongest of bonds.

Sharing the pleasure of humor creates a sense of intimacy and connection between two people⬚ualities that define solid, successful relationships. When you laugh with one another, you create a positive bond between you. This bond acts as a strong buffer against stress, disagreements, disappointments, and bad patches in a relationship. And laughter is contagious just hearing someone laugh primes you to smile and join in on the fun.

Using Humor To Manage And Defuse Relationship Conflict

Conflict is an inevitable part of all relationships. It may take the form of major discord between the two of you or simply petty aggravations that have built up over time. Either way, how you manage conflict can often determine how successful your relationship will be.

When conflict and disagreement throw a wrench in your relationship, humor and playfulness can help lighten things up and restore a sense of connection. Used skillfully and respectfully, a little lighthearted humor canuickly turn conflict and tension into an opportunity for shared fun and intimacy. It allows you to get your point across without getting the other person's defenses up or hurting his or her feelings. For example:

Humor isn't a miracle cure for conflicts, but it can be an important tool to help you overcome the rough spots that afflict every relationship from time to time. Humor— free of hurtful sarcasm or ridicule neutralizes conflict by helping you:

Interrupt the power struggle, instantly easing tension and allowing you to reconnect and regain perspective.

Be more spontaneous. Shared laughter and play, can help you break free from rigid ways of thinking and behaving, allowing you to see the problem in a new way and find a creative solution.

Be less defensive. In playful settings, we hear things differently and can tolerate learning things about ourselves that we otherwise might find unpleasant or even painful.

Let go of inhibitions. Laughter opens us up, freeing us to express what we truly feel and allowing our deep, genuine emotions to rise to the surface.

Managing Relationship Conflict With Humor

Tip 1: Make sure you're both in on the joke

Like any tool, humor can be used in negative as well as positive ways. Making snide, hurtful remarks, for example, then criticizing the other person for not being able to take a joke will create even more problems and ultimately damage a relationship.

Humor can only help you overcome conflict when both parties are in on the joke. It's important to be sensitive to the other person. If your partner, co-worker, family member, or friend isn't likely to appreciate the joke, don't say or do it, even if it's "all in good fun." When the joking is one-sided rather than mutual, it undermines trust and goodwill and can damage the relationship.

Humor should be equally fun and enjoyable for everyone involved. If others don't think your joking or teasing is funny—stop immediately. Before you start playing around, take a moment to consider your motives, as well as the other person's state of mind and sense of humor.

Tip 2: Don't use humor to cover up other emotions

Humor helps you stay resilient in the face of life's challenges. But there are times when humor is not healthy—and that's when it is used as a cover for avoiding, rather than coping with, painful emotions. Laughter can be a disguise for feelings of hurt, fear, anger, and disappointment that you don't want to feel or don't know how to express.

You can be funny about the truth, but covering up the truth isn't funny. When you use humor and playfulness as a cover for other emotions, you create confusion and mistrust in your relationships.

Tip 3: Develop a smarter sense of humor

Some find it easier than others to use humor, especially in tense situations. If your efforts aren't going over well, the following tips may help.

Monitor nonverbal cues. If your partner is not appreciating or enjoying your attempts at humor, you'll be able to tell from his or her body language. Does her smile seem fake or forced? Is he leaning away from you or leaning towards you, encouraging you to continue?

Avoid mean-spirited humor. It may work for some comedians on stage, but used one-on-one, it will not only fall flat but may also damage your relationship. Saying something hurtful or insulting, even when framed as a joke, will alienate the other person and weaken the bond between you.

Create inside jokes. An inside joke is something that only the two of you understand. It can often be reduced to a word or short phrase that reminds you both of a funny incident or amusing story and is usually guaranteed to generate a smile or laugh from the other person. When two people are the only ones "in" on the joke, it can create intimacy and draw you together.

Reasons Why Sharing a Sense of Humor is Key in a Relationship

Making a relationship work takes lots of effort, along with lots of luck. For two people to share a life together, it's necessary that they have certain traits in common; you're not going to enjoy yourself if you can't relate to your partner that well.

Most of us are fairly familiar with the qualities two romantic partners are expected to share if they want to cultivate a fulfilling romance: lifestyle, values, mutual attraction, etc.

However, we often overlook the fact that a similar sense of humor can be a key factor in determining whether or not love will endure. By default, we assume that something as seemingly superfluous as our opinion on what is and is not funny couldn't hold sway over something as significant as our love life.

In truth, though, a shared sense of humor can play a tremendous role in keeping your relationship happy and healthy. Thus;

It Brings Happiness

You don't need a doctor to tell you that life can be stressful. Thankfully, a doctor will tell you that laughter can combat said stress in pretty profound ways. If your partner can help you forget about the pressure you're facing at work, the struggles you're having with family, or the simple unhappiness that strikes all of us on occasion, you're likely to associate that person with good, positive feelings. Whatever your circumstances, knowing that you can go home to someone who makes you feel better will provide for a positive relationship.

You Won't Offend Each Other

It's no secret that we don't all agree on what is funny, or on what subject matter is worthy of a joke. Sometimes, your sense of humor may offend someone. In day-to-day life, this isn't much of an issue. When it comes to your love life, though, it can be pretty important.

You'll Develop A Personal Bond

The odds are good that you share "inside jokes" with some of the people close to you. These moments of shared understanding reflect the fact that the two of you get along in a way that may not be true of all relationships in your life.

Yes, it's a little thing, but in most long-term relationships, the little things are what keep two people interested in one another. If you have the same sense of humor, you'll have inside jokes, and they'll remind you that you love each other.

You Agree On Entertainment

In the age of Netflix, most of us know that we can decompress at the end of the week by having a drink and selecting a sitcom to binge on. It may not seem like much, but if it's what you do to forget about the stressful day that you just had, it plays a major role in maintaining your mental health. On the other hand, if you do share a sense of humor, you can both enjoy Love without wondering if your significant other is merely tolerating it.

You Entertain Each Other

It's a cliché because it's true: If someone can make you laugh on a first date, it's a good sign.

But what about all the subsequent dates? What about the rest of your life? Why is the first date the only instance in which this is important? Wouldn't it be great if your lover could always keep you entertained? If you share a sense of humor, you can probably make this happen. In that way, every single day of the rest of your lives can be, to some degree, just like your first date.

Laughter is like a mini day spa for your emotions

When you're laughing, you're less defensive, you let go of your inhibitions, and are more spontaneous. When you're enjoying a joke or a funny story, you are much more fun to be around. You'll feel more like an Upbeat Ursula than a Debbie Downer.

Humor is crucial when it comes to better communication with your partner

A well-timed joke can lighten a tense situation, and it can help you resolve arguments. Humor can help put things in perspective and assist you in seeing things from your partner's point of view. When you are experiencing the benefits of humor, you loosen up, and you're able to solve a problem more creatively.

Laughter adds excitement to a relationship gone blah

Laughing not only makes us better problem-solvers when there's tension, but it can help us bond us closer together — and increase attraction to our partners. These are all so much more necessary when your relationship feels stale.

Inside jokes between you and your partner will draw you together and add another layer of intimacy to your relationship

When you have a joke that only your partner understand, it can often be a shortcut to closeness. As time goes on, your inside joke can be reduced to a word, a short phrase, or small gesture, the use of which will instantly give the both of you a moment of affection. When you have amusing stories or jokes that just the two of you understand, it's the same as having a secret language. Sure it can be creepy when twins have it, but it's sweet and romantic for you and your significant other.

It's a stress-reliever

Since you're past the stage of trying to impress your partner, and can now just be yourself, sometimes doing a bit of physical comedy, wearing something wacky, or goofing around will lighten things up. It's a great stress reliever for both you and your partner when you release your inner child.

Humor benefits your sex life

There are so many laughable things that can happen when you're having sex; some of them deliberate, and some of them not. If you're relaxed enough to see the humor in the queefing, the farting, and the awkward and unsuccessful role playing, then you can make your bedroom embarrassment one of your inside jokes instead of the most humiliating sex ever.

How to Improve Your Sense of Humor for Your Relationship

If you and your partner would like to find the funny side of your life, here are some tips to help you improve your sense of humor:

Avoid Sweating the Small Stuff: Several years ago I read a fantastic tiny book named Don't Sweat the Small Stuff in Love, which is about many excellent tips to make your relationships happy. One of the best advice in the whole book is just the title of this book: Don't Sweat the Small Stuff. Overlooking the small things and not paying much attention to them will make it much easier to laugh instead of freaking out.

Find Funny Opportunities: Sometimes funny things happen around us, but we miss them. In fact, things which are funny and deserve laughing are always around us. Find such things and spotting them will bring you more reasons to laugh.

Watch Funny Movies with Your Partner: There are lots of marvelous, funny, romantic movies or comedy shows that you can watch together. We love the show The Life and Times of Tim - which makes us burst out laughing every time!

Learn to laugh at yourself: Sometimes we can't realize the funny level of what we had done, or we may feel embarrassed about those things. Yes, we can! We are allowed laughing at ourselves - these embarrassments here, and there aren't that remarkable.

Act in a Goofy Romantic Way: Make a Ways-to-Say-I-Love-You List and get all sorts of crazy ways to express your love. A bar of chocolate, a bowl of breakfast cereal or a lovely handbag - they may be all goofy ways to insert a little pleasure to the relationship. However, don't be afraid to act as silly as a kid sometimes - you'll be surprised what a difference you have made in your in your relationship.

Chapter 8: Funny Inspirations From Everyday Life

Funny Life Quotes are a great way to lift your spirits. When you laugh there are chemicals in the brain that are released that make you feel better? Not only while you are laughing, but the effects last long term. They also reduce blood pressure, and are important in healthy cell formation, among many other benefits.

List of Funny Inspirational Quotes:

"If you don't design your life plan, chances are you'll fall into someone else's plan. And guess what they have planned for you? Not much."

"A sense of humor... is needed armor. Joy in one's heart and some laughter on one's lips is a sign that the person down deep has a pretty good grasp of life." - Hugh Sidey

"A sense of humor is part of the art of leadership, of getting along with people, of getting things done" - Dwight D. Eisenhower

"I consider myself a crayon, I might not be your favorite color, but one day you'll need me to complete your picture".

"Life isn't measured by the number of breaths you take, but by the number of moments that take your breath away."

God, please give me patience, if you give me the strength I will just punch them in the face.

"When I said that I cleaned my room, I just meant I made a path from the doorway to my bed."

"The future is shaped by your dreams, so stop wasting time and go to sleep!

"The sun, with all those planets revolving around it and dependent upon it, can still ripen a bunch of grapes as if it had nothing else in the universe to do." - Galileo Galilei

"Honest criticism is hard to take, particularly from a relative, a friend, an acquaintance, or a stranger." Franklin P. Jones

"There are two ways to pass a hurdle: leaping over or plowing through... There needs to be a monster truck option." Jeph Jacques

"There are two types of people. People who accomplish things, and people who claim to have accomplished things. The first group is less crowded." Mark Twain

"Anyone who takes himself too seriously always runs the risk of looking ridiculous; anyone who can consistently laugh at himself does not." Vaclav Havel

"If we were on a sinking ship, and there was only one life vest... I would miss you so much."

"The most important thing in life is not knowing everything; it's having the phone number of somebody who does!"

"The hardest thing to find in life is happiness - money is only hard to find because it gets wasted trying to find happiness."

"A celebrity is a person who works hard all his life to become well known, then wears dark glasses to avoid being recognized."

"Did you ever notice, whenever you need your keys the most, that's when they're the hardest to find."

"Opportunity is missed by most people because it is dressed in overalls and looks like work" - Thomas Eddison

"If you're going to be thinking, you may as well think big"

-Donald Trump

"Great spirits have always encountered violent opposition from mediocre minds" - Albert Einstein

"Follow your passion, stay true to yourself, never follow someone else's path unless you're in the woods and you're lost, and you see a path then, by all means, you should follow that - Ellen Degeneres

"People often say that motivation doesn't last. Well, neither does bathing – that's why we recommend it daily - Zig Ziglar

"Life always offers you a second chance. It's called tomorrow."

"The great pleasure in life is doing what people say you cannot do."

Life isn't measured by the number of breaths you take, but by the number of moments that take your breath away.

"If you think you are too small to make a difference, try sleeping with a mosquito."

"I always wanted to be somebody, but now I realize I should have been more specific."

"If you're going to be able to look back on something and laugh about it, you might as well laugh about it now."

"I'm bored' is a useless thing to say. I mean, you live in a great, big, vast world that you've seen none percent of. Even the inside of your own mind is endless; it goes on forever, inwardly, do you understand? The fact that you're alive is amazing, so you don't get to say 'I'm bored."

"If you end up with a boring, miserable life because you listened to your mom, your dad, your teacher, your priest, or some guy on television telling you how to do your shit, then you deserve it."

"Good things come to those who wait... greater things come to those who get off their ass and do anything to make it happen."

I'll probably never fully become what I wanted to be when I grew up, but that's probably because I wanted to be a ninja princess.

"Life is a path where we have to enjoy every moment; everyone is going to have the same ending, there is no alternative, so make the most of the time you have now."

"Here is a test to find whether your mission on earth is finished – If you're alive it isn't"

"People were created to be loved. Things were created to be used. The reason the world is in chaos is because things are being loved, and people are being used."

"When one door closes, another opens; but we often look so long and so regretfully upon the closed door that we do not see the one which has opened for us."

"We have no choice of what color we're born or who our parents are or whether we're rich or poor. What we do have is some choice over what we make of our lives once we're here"

"The successful know that the road to success is always under construction; they understand the roughness of it and never expected it to be smooth"

"Goal setting is similar to traveling from point A to point B within a city. If you clearly understand what the goal is, you will definitely reach the destination because you know its address."

"A good laugh overcomes more difficulties and dissipates more dark clouds than any other one thing."

PART FOUR

BECOMING A FUNNIER PERSON

"A good laugh overcomes more difficulties and dissipates more dark clouds than any other one thing."

Chapter 9: Useful Steps On Becoming A Funnier Person

There is no fun to be way too serious in life at every moment; we must not forget life is short enough to take it much seriously. We must enjoy each and every moment we are given and should make it as productive as we can.

Be happy, make others happy and make everyone laugh, do what you love, go for a date, a long drive, get a hobby, and follow your passion, party hard. This will surely make your life much a lot happening.

People who are funny are liked and go well with everyone, and when you and be funny and inspiring at the same time, they can motivate others very efficiently. These people have the capability to convey their message well in a lighter yet efficient manner.

Our sense of humor is not fixed, any more than our smartness. We determine how humorous we are, and we can become funnier if we want. It just takes work and knowing where to start.

Useful Steps On Becoming A Funnier Person

1.Be proficient in your language and develop a good vocabulary

Fumbling for the right words while trying to crack a joke can be embarrassing. It can ruin the funny side of a conversation. Whether it is English, Spanish, Greek or French, being in control of your language and picking the right words should come naturally.

Increase your vocabulary and have a strong grip over your play of words when you are trying to make someone laugh. Using the right words will help you hit the tender, funny bone, whether it is to create ambiguity in meaning, a pun on words or a double entendre.

2.Be confident

If you have low self-esteem, it will severely inhibit your ability to be witty. A lot of people just tell me, "Oh, I'm not clever or witty" -, and I'm telling you to stop thinking that way! Think of yourself as being a newbie at being witty - you might not have the hang of it yet, but the important part is that you're learning!

3.Time your joke to perfection if you want to make others laugh

A good sense of humor and a strong command over language are of little value if the timing of a joke goes wrong. Knowing when to say something is as important as knowing what to say. It is highly situational, so the best way to find out is to learn from experience.

Every time you say something funny in an attempt to make someone laugh, judge the reaction and think "Would it have been funnier if I'd said it earlier/later?" As you make attempts to equip yourself with the skills to be funnier, this deliberate introspection will help you time your humor to perfection.

4.Watch and read funny materials and characters

Analyze what the authors/characters do and how they do it so you can get a feel for their styles and techniques. Take mental notes of what makes you and other people laugh. Do be careful not to copy their material word-for-word, though - you'll just look like an unfunny hack.

5.Remember to pace properly

A properly-delivered joke or witticism gives listeners time to parse, process, and absorb the information they're being given. If you deliver too fast, they'll still be too busy mulling over the setup to properly appreciate the zinger at the end. A proper pause (known as a "beat") is about the time it takes to inhale and exhale once. When it comes to delivering jokes over the Internet, a line or paragraph break can serve the same function as a beat. Go ye forth and watch some funny people to get an idea of how and when beats should be used.

6.Pretend you're a clever/witty character

When you're out and about, get yourself in character for someone who is far more clever and witty than you think you are. You may be surprised how easy being charming and witty suddenly becomes!

Don't reuse your stuff over and over (in front of the same people). If you do this, you'll come off as a one-trick pony and lose pretty much all of your witty creds.

7.Control your expressions and allow others to laugh at your joke

One of the fine abilities of a stand-up comedian is to hold a poker face after saying something hilariously funny while watching everyone burst into fits of laughter. Stand-up comedy would cease to be funny if the comedian himself/herself started rolling with laughter.

Use similar logic in your personal life and try to keep a poker face after trying to be funny. Control your expressions and let the people be entertained with the tickling side of your conversation.

8.Develop a wide knowledge base

Take mental notes of everything, be it history, science, pop culture, etc. so you have a wide variety of potential material to work with. Keep in mind that just about every piece of knowledge you've got is a potential joke or witticism. Likewise, expand your vocabulary - the more words you know, the more words you can play with.

9.Lose inhibitions of speaking to unknown people or a group of people

If your sense of humor is not getting due credit because you are shy of speaking out in front of a group of people, there is no way around it but to lose the inhibition.

Make deliberate efforts to speak out and better yet, plan for a moment when you are going to crack a joke in front of others. As time goes by, the need to plan will decrease, your confidence will increase, and your witty sense of humor will surface by itself.

10.Practice free association

You've probably seen various forums where members played Word Association - one member posts a word, then the next person posts the word the previous word made them think of, and so on and so forth. When possible, practice this on not only words but various random objects and people. What word or words do they make you think of?

11.Display confidence when you crack a joke

When you crack a joke or are going to say something funny, say it loud without too many fumbles and pauses. Carry a confident body language and make sure you get everyone's attention.

Whether or not you can make someone laugh largely depends on whether you believe you can make them laugh or not. Like most other things in life, confidence plays a vital role in your attempt to bring a smile on someone else's face.

12.Don't try too hard to be funny: Humor should come naturally

The ability to make people laugh is something that is cultivated over time and eventually, should come naturally. It is not something that can be picked up overnight. Like a true learner, try to soak up the above tips. Develop a witty sense of humor before you deliberately attempt to crack one joke after another.

13.Watch for loopholes and possible reinterpretations of what people say

In an episode of Lost, several characters were in a very tense situation. One character calmly picked up a book and started reading. Another character asked him, "how can you read?" The first character (◌uite calmly) responded, "my mother taught me."

From the context, we know that the first character was asking "How can you read at a time like this? But the second character, ever a sharp one, spotted a hole in the wording and exploited it for great humor.

PART FIVE

LAUGHTER, HUMOR, AND GOOD HEALTH

Your body cannot heal without play. Your mind cannot heal without laughter. Your soul cannot heal without joy. - Catherine Rippenger Fenwick

Chapter 10: The Relationship Between Laughter, Humor, And Good Health

Laughter is a physical reaction in humans consisting typically of rhythmical, often audible contractions of the diaphragm and other parts of the respiratory system. Laughter is the biological reaction of humans to moments or occasions of humor. It is an outward expression of amusement.

Facts and Figures

•People tend to laugh more when in groups. People should surround themselves with others who laugh because laughter is contagious.

•On average, a child laughs 300 times a day while an adult laughs only 17 times a day.

•Most laughter does not come from listening to jokes; it comes from spending time with family and friends.

•The majority of men report that their laughter is a chuckle, and the majority of women report that theirs is a giggle.

•Adults between the ages of 18 and 34 report laughing the most.

•Smiling is a mild, silent form of laughing.

•Babies start to laugh at about four months of age.

Other Interesting Laughter Information

•Studies from around the world have shown that an atmosphere of humor results in better patient cure, less anesthesia time, less operating time, and shorter hospital stays.

•Laughter is not confined to humans.

Chimpanzees show laughter-like behavior in response to physical contacts, such as wrestling, chasing, or tickling; and rat pups emit short, high-frequency, ultrasonic vocalization during rough-and-tumble play and when tickled.

Rat pups "laugh" far more than older rats.

•Laughter can also make you more attractive to your friends, loved ones, and the opposite sex.

•John Morreall, editor of both Humor: International Journal of Humor Research and The International Journal of Humor and Health, theorizes that human laughter may help inhibit the fight or flight response, making laughter a behavioral sign of trust in one's companions.

•Laughter sounds the same across cultures, leading some researchers to believe that laughter helped bond our ancestors together. In fact, the sound of laughter is so common and familiar that it can be recognized if played backward on tape.

•Laughing burns calories. In fact, laughing for 10 minutes each day can burn the same number of calories as a half-hour workout.

•Laughter can be infectious. It can make others smile and feel happier. We are more likely to remember and want to be around the people who cheer us up and make us laugh.

The Health Benefits of Humor and Laughter

Many people find that maintaining a senseof humor is useful for a goodꝗuality of life. Our sense of humor gives us the ability to find delight, experience joy, and release tension. Additionally, laughter activates the chemistry of the will to live and increases our capacity to fight disease, which makes it an effective self-care tool.

In 1979, Norman Cousins, MD wrote Anatomy of Illness, which brought the subject of humor therapy to the attention of the medical community. In his book, Dr. Cousins details how he used laughter to help ease his pain while undergoing treatment for an incurable and extremely painful inflammation of his body's tissues. As a result, scientific evidence on the effectiveness of humor and its health benefits is now overwhelming.

The following are some of the researched benefits of laughter.

☐   Blood Pressure

People who laugh heartily, on a regular basis, have a lower standing blood pressure than does the average person. When people have a good laugh, initially the blood pressure increases, but then it decreases to levels below normal.

☐   Immune System

Clinical studies by Lee Berk at Loma Linda University have shown that laughter strengthens the immune system by increasing infection-fighting antibodies.

☐   Hormones

Laughter reduces at least four of the neuroendocrine hormones associated with stress. These are epinephrine, cortisol, dopamine, and growth hormone.

☐   Muscle Relaxation

Belly laughs result in muscle relaxation. While you laugh, the muscles that do not participate in the belly laugh relax. After you finish laughing, those muscles involved in the laughter start to relax. Therefore, the action takes place in two stages.

☐   Brain Function

Laughter stimulates both sides of the brain to enhance learning. It eases muscle tension and psychological stress, which keeps the brain alert and allows people to retain more information.

☐   Mental and Emotional Health

Humor and laughter are a powerful emotional medicine that can lower stress, dissolve anger, and unite people in troubled times. The mood is elevated by striving to find humor in difficult and frustrating situations. Laughing at ourselves, and the situation we are in will help reveal that small things are not the earth-shaking events they sometimes seem to be. Looking at a problem from a different perspective can make it seem less formidable for greater objectivity and insight. Humor also helps us avoid loneliness by connecting with others who are attracted to genuine cheerfulness.

•Pain Reduction

Laughter allows a person to "forget" about pains such as those associated with aches, arthritis, etc. In 1987, Texas Tech psychologist Rosemary Cogan used the discomfort of a pressure cuff to test the medical benefits of laughter on pain management. Subjects who watched a 20-minute Lily Tomlin routine could tolerate a tighter cuff than those who had watched an informational tape or no tape at all.

•Respiration

Freᵭuent belly laughter empties your lungs of more air than it takes in, resulting in a cleansing effect – similar to deep-breathing. This deep breathing sends more oxygen-enriched blood and nutrients throughout the body.

•The Heart

Laughter, along with an active sense of humor, may help protect you from a heart attack, according to a study at the University of Maryland Medical Center. The study, which is the first to indicate that laughter may help prevent heart disease, found that people with heart disease were 40 percent less likely to laugh in a variety of situations compared to people of the same age without heart disease.

•A Good Workout

Laughter is the equivalent to "internal jogging."

According to William Fry, MD, Professor of Psychiatry at Stanford University, one minute of laughter is equal to ten minutes on the rowing machine. Laughter can provide good cardiac, abdominal, facial, and back muscle conditioning, especially for those who are unable to perform physical exercise.

Other Benefits - Laughter and humor connect us to other people, foster relationships, rejuvenate and regenerate our energy, and make us feel good!

How You Can Expand Your Sense Of Humor

•Look for the everyday humor. Start looking for the absurd and silly activities that go on around you each day.

•Observe infants and young children learn how to find delight and amusement in the most ordinary things.

•Increase your exposure to comedies, comic sitcoms, joke books, comedy clubs, etc.

•Hang around, funny friends.

•Take a 5 to 10 minute humor break each day. Read jokes, add to a humor notebook, and listen to funny tapes.

•If you hear a joke you like, write it down or tell it to someone else to help you remember it.

•Remind yourself to have fun.

•Spend time with those who help you see the bright side. Whenever possible, avoid negative people.

•Avoid conversations, news, entertainment, etc., that frightens, upsets or distresses you, or makes you feel sad and unhappy.

•Be mindful of just "lightening up."

Chapter 11: What Makes People Laugh?

There are subjects that have the capability to incite laughter to most humans, if now not all. You may have now not mentioned it earlier than, however those gadgets paintings time and time yet again. You are probable to nod in affirmation as you get to every object. Familiarize all of them and try and use them in your journey inside the route of becoming a funnier character.

Pain

All humor is based totally totally on ache, be it emotional or bodily. Take the well-known cool animated film collection "Tom and Jerry", for example. Whenever Jerry hits Tom's foot with a hammer and Tom starts offevolved screaming in pain, the target market jumps in laughter. However, while Jerry hits Tom however Tom isn't harm in any respect, the target market is silent. This is a clean example that inflicting ache to a few different could make humans chuckle. Try to have a look at this in specific well-known humorous suggests, and you could understand it's miles proper.

One shape of humor is an ethnic shaggy dog tale. It is strong because it reasons emotional pain to awesome members of the same institution wherein the amusing is being made. However, take heed that it is ordinary for an ethnic comic tale to get a reaction. When a person punches your nose after telling a humorous story, you have to no longer be amazed because it without a doubt suggests he appreciates your shaggy dog story and returns the choose.

The quality problem approximately the use of pain to cause humor is at the same time as you are the quality subjected to ache. It is definitely no longer humorous at the same time as you get harm. It absolutely does no longer feel proper. If others discover your pain humorous, do now not get disenchanted too much. At least you made people giggle, in spite of the reality which you encountered a calamity. Have you experienced falling down at a pavement or a rocky road and then extraordinary human beings laugh at you? The situation is truly embarrassing, but this certainly indicates ache is an powerful manner to elicit humor.

The Unexpected

When some aspect sudden occurs, that is funny. For instance, if a contestant in an international beauty competition, particularly the Miss Universe, through twist of destiny falls down while walking the ramp, you assume her to sense the ache and get out of the extent at once in humiliation. When she as an alternative gets up proper away and will increase her head in self guarantee, it's far amusing and laudable. Another instance is the decision of some component, much like the decision of the corporation. Some people simply find a misspelled organization name or phrase in a billboard humorous.

If you're making a funny tale, specially in the front of a large audience but no person laughs, a few human beings can also moreover find out it funny. This is because of the reality you do not anticipate this to seem. The nice that you could do in this instance is to snigger out loud in your very very own. Your purpose marketplace is probably put in a clumsy scenario and might move back the choice via guffawing with you too.

Lies

Lies have intrinsic amusing fee. If you are on a queue and also you replied, "I've been right here all of the time" to a person at your lower returned who requested how lengthy you have were given been in line, then he also can discover it funny because it is not actual. In truth, it is an exaggeration. This is exactly why political jokes artwork again and again due to the truth they tell lies concerning liars. Let us take an example. Why is it that politicians run first before they steal cash? Shouldn't or now not it is the alternative manner round? This funny tale works because of the reality a baby-kisser is being in assessment with a robber who steals cash first and runs thereafter.

Another example of lies with a humorous impact is whenever some component is seen in a place in which it want to now not be or is performing some issue in competition to what's commonplace. This type of humorous story is both sudden and humorous, so it has double humor. For example, even as a overweight cool lively movie person which includes Elmer Fudd hides in the again of a small tree, you may discover it humorous. However, if Bugs Bunny does this, you could now not discover humor in it for the motive that he is skinny and small.

Wordplay

Saying some difficulty in a humorous way is a laugh to pay interest. This is why wordplays are very powerful gadget to make humans chuckle on any event. There are many types of wordplays, and taken into consideration one in each of them is while you say a phrase while you're actually thinking about any other. For example, in case your lady buddy calls and you answered through way of addressing her "love" at the same time as your endearment is "sweet," it's miles funny. This is powerful as long as you are making your woman buddy understand that you are honestly joking spherical. Otherwise, it would begin a combat most of the two of you.

Wordplays are greater popularly recounted nowadays as punch traces, and you can see them being used everywhere: on the radio, on social media, in movies, in comedy indicates, and notoriously on tv. Just about any person from all walks of existence is privy to a punch line or that might make you smile, if not snort.

Below are a few extra examples of wordplay:

Question: How to rely quantity cows? Answer: With the usage of a cowculator.

Question: What would probable a blanket say if it falls a ways from mattress? Answer: "Oh, sheet!"

Question: In what way do astronomers throw a party? Answer: Simple. They planet!

Question: Why is it that six is scared of seven? Answer: Because seven ate 9!

Isn't it ironic that your toes fragrance and your nose runs?

The query-and-answer layout of wordplay is a style in recent times, but many other codecs of wordplay are in reality really worth studying.

Puns

Also called paronomasia, puns involve playing on words with similar sounds but splendid meanings. This sort of humor takes gain of the reality that it's far viable to update a phrase with some other phrase of the equal sound, but with virtually one of a type which means. The result might be a brief chortle however the fact is puns are not inherently humorous. You can see puns being applied in a single-liners.

Below are a few examples of puns:

Would you be so inclined to gain the friendship of a plastic fitness care provider?

It is simple to discover if your friends are plastic or not. Put them on the ocean. Whoever sinks is a real pal, and whoever floats is plastic.

I am glad to had been succesful to analyze sign language because of the truth it is relatively available.

Marriage consists of 3 rings: engagement ring, marriage ceremony ring and struggling.

The wooden employee really nailed it, but an idiot screwed the entirety up.

Irony

Irony is a manner this is extensively applied in comedy but is commonly misunderstood as a tool. Irony refers to an instance wherein what surely happens isn't what most anticipate to take place. As stated above, the unexpected provokes laughter.

Take the subsequent examples of irony:

Isn't it worrying to expect that those who keep in mind they are smart frequently use wrong grammar?

I understand I can stop playing every time I want to. I can guess on that.

As I stated earlier than, I'll say this handiest as quickly as.

I had been indecisive in advance than, but nowadays I'm not notable about it.

It is in reality now not my fault if I don't hold myself responsible for my errors.

Sex

If you can manipulate this shape of humor, use it. If now not, stay with it. It is a truth that connection with intercourse can as a minimum located a smile on people's face or supply them a brief giggle. To be capable of use this tactic, be alert all of the time. When someone says some issue, see if you may relate it to sex or eroticism. If so, make a comment on the identical time as keeping the erotic reference in mind. Most human beings might probably recognize the hidden meaning and snigger. If someone says you're being nasty, then you may continuously defend your self via pronouncing you do no longer surely say so.

Sarcasm

This takes area at the same time as you solution a question significantly, even though you clearly stated a few detail very funny. When you use this trick, see that you do it sparingly. If you are not careful, you then definately definately is probably branded as a sarcastic character, which need to no longer be the case. Your purpose is simply to entertain human beings, and you will need to be known as a joker.

Pomposity

If you're keen on looking TV indicates, one reason for that avidness could be the fun price that you get each time you watch those shows. Most TV hosts who make their target market snigger are well cherished by using manner of many. If you watch intently how those hosts behave in their programs, you may locate that other than being sarcastic, they're snobbish or pompous too. When now not completed in extra, pomposity in speech and way is a useful trick to make an target marketplace smile at the least.

Self-deprecation

Though not the awesome manner to initiate laughter, self-deprecation does artwork. You can use this tactic to show a terrible experience into a few issue excellent. This is finished even as you downgrade yourself before each other individual however in a funny way while you likely did a few component wrong.

However, you should exercising caution at the same time as using self-deprecating jokes. Use them best along side your circle of buddies and now not with friends or strangers, who may count on you are prone and function low self-self assure. Also, do now not use this tactic all of the time, or you will lose your appeal.

Chapter 12: How To Be Funny Without Saying A Word?

Apart from telling jokes, you can furthermore make human beings chuckle collectively along with your moves. This is as easy as wearing a shirt posted with funny expenses or figures, putting on a comical facial functions, and dancing even with out song, amongst others. The following are some of the topics you could do to amuse human beings with out announcing a unmarried phrase.

Set the Stage for Laughter

If you are part of a software and you are the keynote speaker, then there are numerous methods so you can lighten up the temper of your target market. You can begin with a fun seen as your target market enters the venue. Another trick is to play cool tune as people begin pouring in. You can inject humor to this device description or the perceive of your presentation itself. Just be innovative.

Facial Expression is Crucial

In a hilarious event in which everybody are guffawing, try and count on a smooth expression as if you are blind to what is taking place round you. When you crack human beings up, their eyes are centered on you. It isn't always a excellent concept to chortle at your very very personal jokes due to the truth you could appear to be a jerk.

Make Fun of Yourself

One manner to enliven any occasion is to make a piece play on your intro. For instance, you could ask the presenter to inform the aim marketplace which you display as much as be the author of 8 books that managed to sell a bit greater than 4 copies. Then have the presenter rectify the mistake with the aid of way of announcing, "Sorry, a slip of the tongue. I mean 4 hundred,000 copies."

Use Objects to Get Some Laughs

It is not unusual statistics that visible aids enhance getting to know. This is especially actual in training, and you may use the same on your talking engagements. Visual aids can assist make your message clear and at the equal time make your target audience snicker. For example, you could show a photograph of balloons to illustrate the way to allow bypass of pressure or a globe to demonstrate that human beings frequently positioned too much burden on their shoulders unnecessarily. As you be aware, visible aids can make your factor clearer and could assist you to inject fun even as you get the hazard.

The backside line

If you are not into humor that lots, then some thoughts cited in this financial smash might probable sound trivial for your particular software program. However, it's far even though satisfactory to find out a manner to up the amusing rate of your talks because it lets in you to rate more than what you typically do. Like what Steve Allen said once, mother and father are possibly to pay extra for amusement than for schooling.

Chapter 13: How To Develop Your Sense Of Humor?

This bankruptcy gives realistic suggestions on growing your sense of humor. This is in that you want to invest most of some time to learn them thoroughly.

Have the Right Emotional State

You ought to analyze a hint mystery that most human beings do not understand approximately being funny and witty, and this is the reality that this capacity is based masses on their emotional u.S. Of america. If you are in a enterprise of buddies, family or associates and if you have the right emotional make-up, then it'd easy as a way to find out strategies to say some issue in a clever way. If you enjoy snug and confident, mind seem to flow glaringly.

On the opportunity hand, if you experience as a substitute concerned and shy in a social putting, then you may discover it difficult to discover clever topics to say. With that type of emotional united states, you cannot assume without delay, have a tendency to stumble and fumble and act awkwardly.

The amazing that you may do on any social occasion is to concentrate on having the right emotional usa. Do now not supply an excessive amount of emphasis at the real phrases you're pronouncing, however on the way you experience within the meantime. When you experience assured, you can without a doubt appearance captivating and attractive.

Always Think out of the Box

In essence, what makes you humorous and witty in a communication is your ability to use progressive and surprising elements of humor while you make a announcement. That is excellent feasible in case you anticipate out of the world.

Thus gaining knowledge of a way to anticipate in this way goes an extended way in growing your fun issue. The simplest manner to make this a reality is to exercising constantly, which you could do both in a social putting or outside.

For example, if someone asks you, "Buddy, are you going to run to the mall? Can you do me a need?" Rather than answering in a predictable style like "Yes, I am," count on for a while and attempt to find out a finer retort. One smart answer is, "Yes, I'm going to the mall, but I'll take a cab. Running gained't get me there rapid." If you check it, that is a little sarcastic, and it is able to offend humans, but if used effectively, it will serve its reason.

Truly Listen

The significance of being a great listener in studying a manner to be funny and funny can not be overemphasized. In order to reply cleverly in any type of communication, you genuinely must pay attention to the messages and phrases conveyed with the useful resource of using precise people.

It is a regarded reality that maximum oldsters do no longer in fact listen. Instead, they're in most times preoccupied with their private thoughts, looking to determine out what they're going to say next, in choice to pay hobby and apprehend what someone else has to say.

In any shape of communique, being a exceptional listener is a prerequisite to being able to assume outdoor the sector. Only after you get the complete message need to you begin thinking about a first-rate reaction.

Do not Put Too Much Pressure on Yourself

In your bid to discover ways to be funny, you need to apprehend that it is not an excellent concept to stress your self to be this sort of person. You can try, but it's going to now not paintings. Your gaining knowledge of need to be fun and gradual, not compelled.

On the alternative, while you stop forcing your self to be funny and permit skip of the need to amuse truely all people, great then will you start feeling cushty and extra confident, letting the a laugh aspect of you return out without trouble.

Most likely, you're subjecting yourself underneath an excessive amount of stress seeking to have an effect on others in social interactions. The great approach is to have a examine social settings as a informal depend and stop taking them very severely. You can easily increase this shape of thoughts-set with a touch exercising.

Remember, gaining knowledge of the artwork of turning into funny and humorous takes time due to the truth it's miles a gadget. The journey entails self-discovery, addiction converting and self-improvement. Constant application of your mastering is the most effective manner to gather the fantastic consequences. Do now not surrender without trouble after your preliminary efforts failed. Keep in mind that the praise of analyzing this potential is significant. You will revel in more assured and happy together along with your social life if you turn into a person with an brilliant humorousness.

Learn from the Expert

As in any form of enterprise, you ought to try and examine a few factor from the professional. These specialists can be everywhere out of your friends, boss, own family, and in particular from expert comedians. The critical interest is that they will be simply exquisite at cracking jokes that rely.

To check from the professionals, try to have a examine how they are announcing or do some thing and hold a check of it. Identify the single issue that makes you respect those humorous humans. Patching up what you examine from anyone and making your plan spherical each funny trait is a exquisite manner to begin your learning. Over time, you will be able to accumulate sufficient strategies from precise people for your arsenal that you could use whenever it's far referred to as for.

Recently, comedy has conquered the podcast worldwide in a fury. The right statistics is that comedy podcasts from tremendous comedians like Joe Rogan and Marc Maron are freely available on-line to really anybody. These podcasts function jokes, hilarious interviews and reminiscences you can down load for your mobile devices and examine from them. Play them anywhere you pass and convey out your amusing issue very quickly.

Watch Funny Shows

At times, a touch concept can help realise your motive quicker. Similar to how the recollections of famous and wealthy people can manual you in accomplishing achievement in existence, searching comedy flicks or standup comedy is one of the notable methods to increase your humorousness.

When you're watching comedy indicates, do now not attention at the funny lines first-class. Note how the comedians carry out on degree, taking a intellectual be aware of every their words and conduct on the equal time as handing over hilarious traces. Besides, being humorous isn't all about the punch lines you are announcing. How you are pronouncing them is equally vital.

Other options to get a hint little bit of perception are movies and tv shows. There are so quite some them which might be overflowing with incredible comedy. For example, the Americans often use physical humor associated with race and intercourse to amuse the target audience, even as the British lease witty jokes often involved with cultural topics. Learning some factor from each worlds let you respect the cultural leanings of each in the direction of sense of humor.

Read and Read Some More

Take maintain of something this is funny and voraciously consume it on your coronary heart's content fabric. Keep in thoughts that chemists study their career thru continuously studying and schooling, in a similar way that sports activities sports writers look at their craft thru writing and studying lots. So it stands to purpose that with a view to end up a funny character, you need to look at plenty and workout what you test.

Among the literature that you should examine are the amusing works via the likes of P.G. Wodehouse, James Thurber, Kaz Cooke, Stephen Fry, Woody Allen, Sarah Silverman, Bill Watterson, Bill Bryson, Douglas Adams, among many others. Children's books written thru high-quality authors are well resources of humor too.

Of direction, studying humorous story books is in your gain. It is not horrible the least bit to memorize a number of the maximum well-known jokes so you can use them when critical. Reading this sort of book might also inspire you to create your very personal jokes and supply them effectively. When analyzing, try to recognize why a specific shaggy dog story is a high-quality one. In the same manner, attempt to recognize why others do no longer paintings.

Use Fake Stories

You do not have to inform true memories to elicit laughter from your audience. In truth, comedians utilize fabricated testimonies to generate immediate laughter. One instance is Brian Regan's the usage of the "Stupid in School" humor to make such amusing. Though the story is not proper, the goal marketplace responds to it honestly again and again all once more. As you can see, it is so easy to tickle the bones of your target market.

Associate with a Jolly Company

Make friends and socialize with buddies whom you positioned are a laugh to be with. It isn't uncommon information that enthusiasm is contagious. Keeping a business enterprise with happy people can remodel your outlook in existence in a first rate manner. By spending time socializing with folks who constantly find the sunny element of existence, you may have the proper emotional country to turn out to be a funny fellow. In addition, you will be able to take in the fashion of your friends as regards to turning in their witty traces.

Practice your Jokes Safely

Your humorousness will decorate over time with consistent exercising, but make certain to exercising in a stable environment at the begin and circulate on later to a far broader target audience as your functionality improves. This steady surroundings can be your circle of buddies and your family. If you are making a mistake, then those human beings are much more likely to forgive you and provide advantageous criticisms to beautify your expertise.

On the other hand, in case you exercising in the office, your body of workers or your colleagues also can furthermore experience uneasy with the sudden exchange in your individual. Of path, a larger target audience expects you to supply your traces perfectly from the get-bypass. A suitable manner to begin is to exercise with people whom you believe.

Work on your Accent

You need to recognize now not pleasant at the same time as to speak at the same time as talking to humans however furthermore whilst to prevent. A humorous person isn't like a parrot who talks masses constantly all the time. You additionally need to paintings to your accessory to grow to be a nicely-rounded, funny guy. It is a reality that what is executed right is interesting and what's completed incorrect is top notch. Often comedians make errors on cause to make humans chortle. However, if you make a mistake with the resource of hazard and also you do now not recognize the manner to get higher, then that may be a hassle considering that which could positioned you in an inept function.

It is a incredible idea to workout your pronunciation first earlier than you attempt to make a show somewhere. One way to gain that is to study a ebook or newspaper aloud to yourself every day. A excessive fellow can tell a funny tale and get a chortle, but a clearly a laugh fellow can tell the equal shaggy canine tale and get amusing. As said before, what you're announcing is one detail and the way you assert it's far every one of a kind. A humorous man normally has splendid accent.

Chapter 14: How To Make Your Witty Lines Count

Being a amusing fellow does not endorse telling jokes usually or performing like a clown. All it takes is a actually happy coronary heart and the sensitivity so that you can provide you with funny subjects out of nowhere, the use of the matters or situations which is probably occurring around.

The following is the type of character which you need to anticipate everywhere you circulate a good way to deliver your punch lines at a second's be conscious. The ultimate aspect gives easy procedures you may use whilst trying to find to maintain your witty lines.

Be observant

Many comedians make tens of tens of millions of bucks the use of a easy trick referred to as observational humor. One such comic is Jerry Seinfeld. He is so particular at cracking jokes out of every day reviews and occurrences. Though having a big type of know-how will increase your functionality for humor, having a eager eye to see the world at huge is more crucial. In fact, severa informed human beings may additionally additionally forget about the a laugh a part of subjects. A funny character would not allow humor come to skip without doing justice to it. The diffused humor sitting proper in advance than your eyes often gives the maximum impact.

Be an high-quality listener

When in a communication, it's miles truly beneficial to pay interest closely to the people you're speakme to and honestly understand what they are pronouncing. Despite your talent at cracking jokes, you may continually test from unique humans. There are continuously assets you do now not recognize, so be prepared to pay attention. Listening to others makes you no longer simplest a wittier character, but additionally a practical character to narrate with.

Be mysterious

As people begin to recognize you as a a laugh man or woman, they will certainly count on you to present a smart remark to anything stated with the useful resource of someone else. However, you do now not have to be that form of character. Adding a hint of unpredictability in your wittiness may want to make you a really cool and clever man or woman.

Sometimes even if you do now not say something and also you simply show a smile, people round you will in all likelihood start laughing. This is because they expect something humorous is on foot in your mind. If you virtually have mounted a reputation as a a laugh individual, then it'll make an extended-lasting impact. Even if you are excessive at coping with a meeting, as an example, your buddies and pals will even though chuckle at you because they understand who you're.

In addition, there may be an element of unexpectedness within the way you deal with yourself, so they may discover your attitude a laugh. More possibly, they are equipped as a manner to throw a line or ultimately of your speech.

When you're within the agency of your pals, you do now not need to begin a humorous tale all the time. You can notwithstanding the truth that liven up the get-together with the aid of commenting some factor humorous to a observation given with the aid of the usage of a person else. If you have got one-of-a-type recommendations up your sleeve to inject fun into the meet-up, then use them through manner of turns. The key here is you do now not act too predictably on your technique.

Be Yourself

Live your life in a fun manner thru inclusive of humor, but see to it that you do now not faux to be someone else. This can be the worst trap you can fall into in your try and be a humorous man. If your herbal demeanor is a immoderate one, you do not must be a talkative fellow. Be who you're and surely add spice to your life through way of having a extra excellent and fun outlook.

Know your Environment

Be observant of your environment. Funny folks are informed of cutting-edge affairs, and that they've a way to explicit facts in a smart way. You do no longer ought to be an idiot who's privy to not anything but crack jokes right right right here and there. Instead, be a practical individual who is privy to what goes on around you.

Think Positive

Having a high-quality outlook approximately lifestyles in general is an vital thing of being a witty and amusing individual. Remember, as said in advance, your emotional country could make or smash you because of the truth the funny man round the corner. Be fine about life and attempt to see things in a excellent mild.

Think Funny

To end up a humorous man or woman, it is going without pronouncing which you need to count on a completely unique paradigm. This refers to the way you take a look at the arena. If you typically attempt to examine the brighter aspect of existence, then your sense of humor will waft spontaneously. To be capable of see the fun topics inside the good deal, you want to not take topics too critically. Think of glad thoughts and take topics extra casually.

Have a Joyful Laugh

Someone who contains a heat smile and a pleasant chuckle whilst meeting with antique and new buddies alike can go away an have an effect on that he's a fun and likeable individual to be with. If you must turn out to be a funnier character, then you truely must be visible as an agreeable and amusing fellow.

Add Variety

When in a verbal exchange with a company of friends, attempt to add variety to the topics of debate. Otherwise, the communicate will become dry and tiresome. If you consider you studied you have got dealt too prolonged in a single difficulty, then try to contact new ones and hold the communication alive.

Use the Rule of Three

One form of humor that stands the take a look at of time is called the guideline of thumb of 3. This humor consists of three layers. While the primary layers make up ordinary, normal and predicted topics, the zero.33 layer is pulled out of skinny air. This 1/3 layer is wherein a laugh is made. The easy form of the rule of thumb of thumb of three is going some element like this: "For these days, my plans are to easy my room, wash my garments, and walk the dinosaur." The 1/3 object inside the collection is sudden, which, as has been mentioned in advance, is an effective device to generate laughs.

Use Callbacks

Have you placed that numerous comedians have the dependancy of bringing again antique jokes and pronouncing them in a one-of-a-kind way and with a brand new attitude on a brilliant occasion? You can see they get big laughs the second one time round. This technique is known as a callback. If you locate that a shaggy dog tale works at one time, then it might art work at all all over again. So attempt to convey it lower lower back later, but it in a diffused manner. As a rule of thumb, a callback have to now not be used greater than 3 times on any individual occasion.

Re-create Other Jokes

Interesting one-liners can offer you with many punch traces that you may use at your disposal. In addition, they may assist you image out conditions on your existence a terrific deal better. It isn't crucial which you memorize loads of punch lines. Just get the records of what passed off in your elegance or at a bar, and then relate the tale whilst a comparable revel in takes region on your actual life.

Borrow a Few Cunning Lines

If you haven't created your personal jokes, then you may use the witty strains of famous authors to enliven your talks. Some awesome resources of funny expenses are the Internet, television, films, books, magazines and newspapers. One deliver of particular significance is Reader's Digest. When borrowing prices from first-rate human beings, make sure that those fees are not too famous, in any other case some humans can also logo you as a copycat.

Do now not Chuckle at your Own Jokes

This has been noted at different factors on this e-book, but it is without a doubt well well worth bringing up once more right right here because you want to make your witty lines matter. Laughing at your private jokes isn't always honestly beneficial. This can also even go away an have an impact on that you are an newbie.

Chapter 15: Things To Consider At The Equal Time As Delivering Your Lines

There are a few vital additives within the a achievement delivery of humor. Make sure to pay attention to these items at the same time as you try and placed on a show. As mentioned in advance than, what you say is one thing and the way you're pronouncing it's miles a few one of a kind, so the transport of your witty strains is going an extended way with regards to turning into a absolutely a laugh individual.

Audience

Different types of people snigger at diverse things. For a few human beings, satire motives them to snicker. For others, sensationalism does the trick. Thus, it's miles vital to tailor your humor to a selected target audience.

Not everybody can recognize the feeling of being a millionaire, driving a helicopter or having a little one. Yet clearly absolutely everyone is aware of the manner it feels to crave for coins, pass fast and love someone clearly. In this case, you could play with fundamental human feelings to cover more ground for your humor.

When you are in a organisation of strangers, find out what subjects they will be maximum interested by and what tickles their bones. For example, if the ones people aren't the scholarly kind, possibly cheap jokes or perhaps avenue jokes will art work. It is probably less difficult to make human beings snigger if you realize them better.

If you're making a speech to a massive goal marketplace of tremendous humans, then your act should no longer insult them by way of the use of manner of throwing reasonably-priced jokes. So it's far vital to preserve in thoughts whether or not the occasion is formal or now not. If you need to hold a message, ensure your comedian tale receives the message across in a fun and clever manner.

Timing

As the saying is going, strike whilst the iron is heat. When you try to be funny, timing is an critical trouble. Being able to count on fast is a useful abilities which you want to nurture. If you believe you studied too slowly whilst searching for to offer you with a comedian tale, the hilarious 2d may bypass by means of manner of. When the humor is introduced too late, it would now not get the popular effect, so react short and in no manner allow an opportunity depart.

Comebacks, or one-liners, are a laugh. A character says some detail now not humorous in itself, and you're making a commentary that makes the announcement humorous. In this case, timing is so vital. For the humor to be effective, your response want to be brief and complete. For instance, absolutely one in all your pals talks about hair and says some element in the following line, "Isn't it bizarre that hair awesome grows in regions: at the pinnacle and within the pubic region?" At this factor, your pal is certainly growing a announcement likely out of nowhere and does now not assume an answer. You quipped, "Just talk for your self." This retort is incredible to provoke laughter on the same time as the use of the message home.

If the timing is off, then it's miles quality now not to attempt creating a shaggy canine tale at all. Your window of opportunity is limited, so you must react short. If the threat has handed, then simply permit it bypass. You gets a few different chance sooner or later.

The worst that you could do while searching out to be funny is pull pranks or crack jokes during weddings, funerals and locations of worship. You is probably charged of disrespect and be hated for that. A certainly fascinating fellow is someone with humor and sensibility.

Pacing

An accurate transport of witticism or joke allows the target market a while to investigate, gadget and recognise the message being conveyed. If you deliver a punch line right now after another, then the impact of the second one humor might be misplaced in confusion because of the truth the listener continues to be busy seeking to apprehend the preceding one.

As a brand new rule, the right pacing, additionally referred to as the beat, is someplace close to the c language among breathing in and exhaling as soon as. When you write jokes at the Internet, ensure to embody a line smash or , which serves the function of a beat. To discover ways to use beats successfully, watch humorous indicates and find out how comedians pace themselves on the same time as turning in their witty strains.

Chapter 16: Good And Bad Types Of Humor

Different styles of humor exist around us, from puns to irony to satire. All of them are excellent so long as they generate the intended response. To ensure your jokes make a distinction in humans's lives, you need to recognize in which to attract the road among correct and bad humor.

Good Types of Humor

Good humor attracts humans closer to you and makes the connection even stronger and the company greater fun. You have no fear of being hated, so that you do no longer have to be to your protect at the same time as you socialize with others.

Childish Humor

Childish jokes are stupid property you do to others and vice versa. As lengthy as childish humor is finished cautiously, it can be fun and can construct dating, especially among siblings and fanatics. Examples of childish humor consist of calling humans stupid names, making someone inhale your flatulence, and hiding a person else's slippers somewhere, among others. This shape of humor works good-bye because it is not malicious.

Situational Humor

Situational humor is one of the most commonly used sorts of humor. It is completed with the useful resource of setting characters in a humorous state of affairs. How the characters react to this case is the deliver of fun. If you're acquainted with the term "sitcom," it comes from the terms "situational" and "comedy." Often characters display strong reactions to even trivial topics, making the scenes funnier.

Bitchy Humor

This form of humor is frequently mean and nasty. Since bitchy humor is insulting at times, you want to apply it with warning. See to it that you do now not use this sort of humorous story even as in a company of strangers, in any other case you can get into trouble.

Here are a few examples of bitchy humor:

Beautiful women are seldom unfastened, and loose ladies are seldom lovely.

Question: Is this seat empty? Answer: Yes, and this one too if you sit down there.

That disturbing instant at the same time as you certainly inform the reality, however no man or woman believes you due to the truth you're guffawing.

If you are not a properly-rounded joker, then stay faraway from bitchy humor so that you can keep away from offending humans and making enemies in region of pals.

Practical Humor

Practical humor is a naughty trick being achieved to others, resulting in perplexity, embarrassment, discomfort or confusion. Someone who executes realistic humor is referred to as a sensible joker. Other names for sensible humor are gag, prank, shenanigan or jape.

You can see this form of humor anywhere, specifically on television and social media. One instance is at the same time as people are on foot down the road in a silent night after which a daunting determine seems on the corner. These humans then start strolling in particular recommendations out of worry, and the target market nearly fall off their seats at the same time as guffawing. Practical humor works because it motives pain.

Bathroom Humor

Otherwise known as relaxation room humor or scatological humor, relaxation room humor refers to crude humor that gives with urination, defecation, vomiting and flatulence. Often it's also sexual jokes. You can use this kind of humor while no man or woman is aware of the solution to a question. For instance, if a person asks why Bruce Lee died and because of the truth there's no account of the real purpose of his lack of existence, you could say he died of trouble defecating after attending a party. This kind of grimy jokes works so long as you do no longer use it whilst humans are accrued spherical to eat.

Take-It-Easy Humor

When any person is feeling down, one way to cheer him up is to apply take-it-smooth humor. This is finished via the use of sharing your very very own humorous, awkward tale at the same time as you encountered a comparable situation and the way you screwed up in that second. It is exquisite to apply this form of humor in case you intend to loosen up an awkward scenario. The quit end result is that you make human beings experience better, this is a splendid way to construct friendship.

Bad Types of Humor

If you want to be a funny character, it is feasible for you to say some thing you need; but, you need to no longer pass the street amongst being funny to being advise. The following are the horrible kinds of humor you want to be privy to and try to avoid the least bit costs.

Condescending Jokes

Never make amusing of all of us in a set on your try and make human beings snigger.

It would likely work on the begin, but in the long run, others can also start feeling awkward and examine you as a merciless individual. Standup comedians are first rate at using this form of humor, but it does no longer endorse it's far right for all of us.

Mimicry

Imitating how a pal acts while he isn't around can be amusing inside the starting. However, different human beings might likely get weary of you and notice you as an average person who does not care approximately the feelings of others. Mimicry works high-quality if the individual you're ridiculing is round and has the risk to guard himself and imitate you too.

Cocky Humor

Cocky humor can be powerful if now not carried out in extra because it suggests you have were given self guarantee in yourself. However, in case you go too a ways, people spherical you will probably get aggravated along aspect your overconfidence. You are seeking to undertaking a fascinating character, no longer a cocky one. You ought to try to avoid the usage of this humor alongside side your associate too. For instance, if she says, "Do I look all right?" and also you replied, "Of route, you do; except, you are with me." Do now not be too complete of yourself.

Flawed Humor

If there is some factor you do no longer like about a person, it is higher to be sincere about it via pointing it out to the individual. Never use a shaggy dog story to bring the flaw to his interest. For example, if a pal has a lousy breath, don't say, "Did you eat lifeless rat these days"? That is form of a punch inside the face, that can have lasting repercussions in your courting with the man.

Picky Humor

Picky humor is similar to bullying. This occurs at the identical time as you crew up with others to tease any other man or woman. It might in all likelihood experience funny to you, however to the opportunity fellow, he is going to feel lonely, prone and miserable. Of unique observe, never make a laugh of a woman's flaw. Remember, girls are very emotional. They find it difficult to transport on from an embarrassing second. Even a slightly terrible comment can gravely have an effect on the feeling of a female, so be cautious.

Chapter 17: Friendship

Friendship is a kind of relationship based totally on a mutual affection amongst or greater people. Its foundation is more on inter-private bond amongst human beings in choice to through manner of smooth affiliation.

Friendships are available in masses of considered one of a kind paperwork, sizes and styles. You can be pals with every person you want. In truth, there are times at the same time as you come to be pals with humans you least expected you'll be friends with.

Although there loads of methods to make buddies, it's far brilliant to begin making friends with humans to whom you may percentage commonplace interests with.

So earlier than further discussing a way to begin making friends, proper here are smooth steps in starting a friendship which you must understand about:

Step 1: Meet People

Since friendship is a relationship to be shared via or more people, the first step that you want to do is to exit and meet as many human beings as you could. You can try this thru following what pursuits you. Don't hesitate to enroll in social golf equipment, sports activities activities corporations or possibly non secular corporations. You can also meet humans via manner of attending community gatherings or activities that encompass social interaction. Try to sign up for activities that meet often as it will suggest which you'll be meeting the identical humans time and again all over again, for that reason growing the chances of making new friends. This step may additionally additionally moreover take time with a purpose to set up a connection or rapport with feasible friends, so ensure to actively take part in all of the matters the group can be doing that permits you to get to comprehend them higher and vice-versa.

Step 2: Start a Conversation

For you to expose people that you can make an incredible buddy, the following step you want to do is to start a pleasant verbal exchange. During the communication, it's miles crucial that you display that you are a exquisite listener and that you are in fact worried inside the people you are speaking to. You can do this via constantly making eye contact on the identical time as speaking. Also, ensure which you supply relevant remarks and ask the right questions. Lastly, don't forget to grin all the time.

Step 3: Do Stuff Together

The final step in beginning a friendship can be finished satisfactory after a connection has been made. Once you've got installed a bond, you want to now increase the friendship to the following level. How? Encourage your destiny friends to do stuff collectively out of doors your comfort quarter. But ensure that the topics that you and your buddies can be doing are subjects that you all love to do. You can't strain what you need for your buddies so it is important that you first ask them what form of stuff they want to do.

Chapter 18: Make A Good First Impression

When making pals, one of the maximum crucial activities is to make a great have an effect on of your self. And when you say accurate have an impact on, it literally and figuratively manner being capable of "galvanize" humans in a "correct" manner. For people to love you and really need you to be blanketed of their circle of friends, you have were given to show them which you are certainly buddy-material.

But making an tremendous affect is tons less complicated stated than accomplished because of the fact you wouldn't need to overdo impressing human beings. The great manner to move is to behave as herbal as you are and virtually be yourself all the time.

Here are some topics that can help you in making an high-quality first have an effect on for your friends:

1. Always be on time. If you're to meet someone for the number one time, it's far a want to that you don't be overdue. If feasible, try and be the first one to reach. Being on time manner that you are interested by meeting that person.

2. Just be your self. You received't be developing a extremely good first impact if you can strain your self to have an effect on someone whom you're assembly for the first time. Just be yourself. Don't faux to be someone you are not.

three. Present yourself as it must be. To make a incredible first have an effect on, physical look topics. Since the character whom you're assembly for the primary time has no idea of who you are or what shape of man or woman you've got, the manner you look is the primary clue that he or she has on you. But this doesn't advocate that you need to appear like a movie star to create a extremely good impression. All you need to is to offer yourself correctly. Presenting your self efficiently doesn't simplest embody the garments you'll be wearing however your over-all demeanor as nicely. So make certain to provide your self as it need to be always.

four. Always placed on a triumphing smile. There's a announcing this is going some element like this, "Smile and the arena smiles too." So in growing an top notch first have an effect on, not a few thing beats a triumphing smile. Be wonderful to greet every body with a real smile and in reality they may smile lower returned at you.

5. Be confident. It is ordinary with a purpose to get anxious while assembly any person for the primary time. Sometimes, this anxiety often outcomes in concerned conduct and sweaty arms. So what you want to do is to manipulate your feeling of

being nervousness. This may be achieved with the useful resource of believing in your self. How are you able to be anxious when you have self belief inner you?

6. Be exquisite. Having a pleasant outlook in life is continuously a first-rate thoughts-set to have. If you've got got had been given a excessive best mind-set, all of the negativity can be blocked. Your exceptional thoughts-set will display within the entirety and a few component you do. Projecting a fantastic thoughts-set, despite the fact that faced with complaint, commonly give up give up result to a superb first impact.

They say that first impressions final. That is actual. That is why it is very vital that each one friendships begin on the proper foot.

Most of the instances, what human beings take into account you the primary time they see you remains in their reminiscences for quite some time. And even though it's miles viable that their first have an effect on of you can trade when they get to recognize you greater, it is constantly higher that friendships begin on a first rate way.

But giving a brilliant first have an effect on is exquisite half of of the struggle due to the fact the actual venture is a manner to keep it. For example, if people's first have an effect on of you is which you're a accountable individual, it's miles crucial which you be accountable inside the entirety and some aspect you do, especially even as you are together with your pals due to the reality they assume you to be one.

Chapter 19: Be Interestingly Funny

So what kind of first effect can be taken into consideration an remarkable form of first have an effect on? Well, it absolutely relies upon on your man or woman. As they are announcing, what you be aware is what you get so simply be right to your self, and with a bit of luck human beings will discover ways to accept you for who you sincerely are.

But if there's one aspect which could make an wonderful first impact to most humans, it is through manner of having an seemingly humorous persona. Being seemingly funny manner being capable of make humans spherical you want you through laughter.

Being interesting and funny are unique personalities. You ought to have an exciting persona however it doesn't normally recommend that you'll be humorous as well and vice-versa.

So being "apparently humorous" calls for plenty greater than surely having the capacity to crack a comedian tale or two. You need to have a persona that people can be interested by knowing. To be humorous, you need to think about yourself as a person who plays to your friends, like how a performer makes his or her purpose marketplace giggle. In exclusive terms, you want to be the lifestyles of the organization. Also, in an effort to be "curiously funny", it's far a want to that you recognize yourself first. And this e-book will train you what tendencies capability pals will surely discover exciting in you.

If you need to be interesting to your pals, proper right here are some thoughts that will let you along the way. First issue to recognize approximately being interesting is ready introducing people to new subjects. If you need to make buddies with humans you've met for the number one time, it'll assist if you can introduce them to matters that they possibly don't apprehend. People will discover you thrilling when you have the knowledge or facts that they would love to have, but don't haven't begun.

For people to see you as an exciting person, stay a a laugh existence as viable. Being thrilling isn't quite an entire lot prepared at your home before simply assembly on the facet of your buddies. Being exciting is set dwelling a fun and thrilling existence. Try to end up the form of person who constantly has new topics to reveal to each person. If you're a laugh to be with, human beings will clearly want to make buddies with you.

Another way to be an thrilling individual is studying to offer what you need to mention in an thrilling way. Two people must have the identical story to mention however how they are saying it in some different manner makes the story extra thrilling. One can tell the story proper away-ahead missing the emotion required to make the story enticing. While the second can tell the tale with sufficient electricity, making the story lots less dull and similarly unique.

Having an thrilling persona furthermore manner growing an instinct for things that human beings ought to want to pay attention. This is self-explanatory; no man or woman cares about topics that don't interest them. It is unnecessary to say some thing to every other man or woman who doesn't appear to care to listen what you want to mention. This is why it's miles critical that you realise who you're speaking to so you can adjust what you need to mention to what she or he might possibly need to pay interest. For instance, if you are trying to begin a communication with a person who likes basketball, don't attempt to speak about stuff about the solar machine. Try to begin the communication via talking about topics that has something to do with basketball.

Lastly, being exciting is all about your being specific and one of a kind from absolutely everyone else. Simple not unusual sense dictates that how are you going to be thrilling to others if you have nearly the identical matters to day or to do just like the rest of them. Being interesting method which you have a few element that simplest you can provide.

Chapter 20: Be Memorable

Be memorable can advise masses of factors however one smooth and easy definition of being memorable is making humans miss you every time you are not spherical. It is having a shape of man or woman that sticks to the minds of human beings you meet.

Friends need to now not forget about approximately you after assembly you for the number one time. Giving an excellent first effect is right, however giving a long lasting authentic impact is better.

One powerful way, of making your future buddies take into account you, is to depart them with a "mark" of your character. It can be the manner you talk, the way you snigger or the manner you smile. It must be some element that is extensively yours - some issue as a way to remind them of you all the time.

Always consider that the most critical element to take be aware whilst assembly people for the number one time is to truly be yourself, and now not act like someone else. Don't try and play a function because it will honestly seem that you're trying so difficult to have an effect on.

As the saying goes, "Don't sincerely be your self. Instead, be the fantastic feasible model of your self." This truly technique that for people to don't forget you, strive to reveal them all of the quality subjects approximately you.

One manner of creating humans not neglect you is by the use of getting them to chuckle. Try to observe a comedy movie and you could display to your self that whenever you recollect a humorous scene in the film, you can't assist but to chortle. This is due to the fact happy thoughts are usually much much less complex to go through in thoughts than sad mind.

In making friends, if you supply them the primary have an effect on that you are the shape of man or woman who exudes happiness and a jolly man or woman. For positive, no character will overlook you.

Chapter 21: Learn To Listen

Another accurate trait to have with a purpose to make friends is having the ability to be an tremendous listener. Being a outstanding listener manner you're sensitive to the wants and needs of the human beings you engage with.

Nobody desires to be friends with someone who doesn't comprehend on the same time as to save you talking and start listening. Learning to pay attention could be very vital for a friendship to prosper as it gives you the possibility to analyze extra approximately your pals.

Being an amazing listener dreams you to have two traits. First one is sensitivity while the second one is staying strength.

A literal definition of sensitivity is being sensitive to subjects which are taking place round you. But in listening, sensitivity is the ability to react correctly at some stage in fantastic situations. Being touchy way data while to pay attention and while to speak.

For example, if you have a chum who wants to confide to you a problem about his or her love existence, you need to be sensitive sufficient to pay hobby for your friend as she or he vents all her disappointments and frustrations. You need to now not try and offer advices, until your friend asks to your recommendation.

On the opportunity hand, persistence, moreover referred to as forbearing, is being capable of undergo tough situations, due to this having the capability to persevere even as provoked. Simply described, staying strength is being able to live calm and accrued even if beneath pressure. When it consists of listening, staying electricity in fact technique know-how even as, what and the manner to react at the same time as confronted with one in every of a kind conditions.

In making pals, learning to pay attention is essential because it the nice manner we get to apprehend humans. In fact, listening is considered as one of the maximum vital, if not the most crucial skills that you have to have. How well you are in listening can also have a incredible effect at the pleasant of friendships you'll have with people.

Through listening, we are able to attain vital data about our buddies. We can studies topics we have to realize approximately them; each the first-rate and the awful. This information can assist us in coping with our friends in a few unspecified time inside the future of nicely and horrible times.

Another advantage of being a first rate listener is getting to apprehend human beings. If you don't be aware of what people will say, there can be a chance that you may now not understand their personalities altogether.

Listening also consequences to having a feeling of amusement. If you don't get bored listening, it manner that you are virtually taking element in what you're taking note of. Listening to what your buddy has to mention, regardless of how trivial it's miles, is an important part of retaining a healthful and inexperienced friendship.

Chapter 22: Your Body Language

By definition, body language is a shape of non-verbal communique. It is a manner of expressing what human beings experience or need to say through their physical conduct.

Body language may be expressed via body posture, facial expressions, hand gestures and eye movements.

Generally-talking, body language is a sub-aware behavior thru nature making it simply unique from a few unique form of non-verbal communique, called signal language, that is an intentional act of conversation done via a aware individual.

Body language can provide pointers or clues as to the actual united states of thoughts of an person. It can also supply an idea on what the over-all mind-set of the character is. Body language can recommend boredom, pleasure or maybe intoxication. An intoxicated person who says he's sober can't disguise the truth about his actual condition. Even if he says that he isn't intoxicated, the way he talks and walks says in any other case.

Body language could be very vital in relationships and communication. And regardless of the truth that frame language is not spoken, it may still reveal many things about one's actual emotions to different people and the way those humans absolutely screen how they experience toward you.

Understand that body language is a very crucial device in conversation that constitutes fifty percent of what human beings attempt to say with different people. So if you want to recognize how to talk efficiently using your body, it's miles just proper to recognize how you may and may't do together with your frame to say what you want to say.

The vital issue to recognize in frame language is figuring out what type of messages or symptoms you are attempting to send. Our bodies may be likened to walking advertisements that display our inner feelings and mind. So while the usage of body language as a way of speakme with pals, constantly make sure that you are sending the right signs. This can be very essential due to the truth how your body behaves says hundreds about what you need to mention or want to do.

Clear examples of frame language that you may use to pals are a smile and a hug. Smiling is the most effective but best manner of speakme in a non-verbal way. You don't have to mention how glad you are seeing a friend or how thankful you are to a incredible deed that a chum has completed for you.